Power, politics

Manchester University Press

Power, politics and influence at work

Tony Dundon, Miguel Martínez Lucio, Emma Hughes, Debra Howcroft, Arjan Keizer and Roger Walden

Manchester University Press

Published by Manchester University Press
Altrincham Street, Manchester M1 7JA
www.manchesteruniversitypress.co.uk

British Library Cataloguing-in-Publication Data
A catalogue record for this book is available from the British Library

ISBN   978 1 5261 4641 0 paperback

First published 2020

Typeset by Newgen Publishing UK
Printed in Great Britain
by TJ International Ltd, Padstow

Contents

List of figures   vi
List of tables   vii
About the authors   viii
Foreword   ix
List of abbreviations   xiii

1   Work, power and politics   1

2   History, global capitalism and contexts   17

3   The state, law and equality   44

4   Who speaks for whom at work?   76

5   Work and future contexts   99

Employment law cases   116
Bibliography   117
Index   147

Figures

1.1 Bases of power (source: French and Raven, 1959)   4
1.2 A virtuous circle of solidarity (source: Doellgast *et al.*
    (2018: 13), reproduced with permission of Oxford
    Publishing Ltd.)   8
1.3 A vicious circle of solidarity (source: Doellgast *et al.*
    (2018: 18), reproduced with permission of Oxford
    Publishing Ltd.)   9
1.4 Efficiency, equity and voice framework
    (source: adapted from Budd (2004))   12
2.1 Temporary employees as a share of total
    employment, 2007–2018 (source: Eurostat
    (https://ec.europa.eu/eurostat; lfsq_etpga))   29
2.2 Part-time employment as a share of total
    employment, 2007–2018 (source: Eurostat
    (https://ec.europa.eu/eurostat; lfsa_eppga))   30
2.3 NSFE as a share of total employment UK, 2007–2018
    (source: adapted from UK Office for National
    Statistics (www.ons.gov.uk/; EMP01 & EMP17))   32
2.4 Involuntary character temporary employment
    ('could not find a permanent job'), 2007–2018 (source:
    Eurostat (https://ec.europa.eu/eurostat; lfsq_etpga-2))   35
4.1 Equality/inequality ratios (D9/D1) and collective
    bargaining coverage (2016 or latest available)
    (source: Grimshaw and Hayter (2020: 161), using
    ILOSTAT and OECD.Stat)   87

Tables

1.1   Structure of the book   15

2.1   Earnings of temporary workers as a share of earnings of permanent workers (2014)   36

4.1   Scope of joint consultative committees (percentages)   80

4.2   Union forms, levels and possible outcomes   82

4.3   Issues union reps spend their time on (percentages)   83

About the authors

Tony Dundon is Professor of Human Resource Management (HRM) and Employment Relations, Kemmy Business School, University of Limerick, Ireland; and Visiting Professor, Work and Equalities Institute, University of Manchester, UK.

Debra Howcroft is Professor of Technology and Organisation, Work and Equalities Institute, University of Manchester. Debra is an editor of *New Technology, Work and Employment*.

Emma Hughes is a lecturer in HRM at the University of Liverpool Management School. Emma is a member of the British Sociology Association.

Arjan Keizer is Senior Lecturer in comparative HRM and industrial relations in the HRM, Employment Relations and Employment Law Group, Work and Equalities Institute, University of Manchester.

Miguel Martínez Lucio is Professor in the HRM, Employment Relations and Employment Law Group, Work and Equalities Institute, University of Manchester. Miguel is an editor of *New Technology, Work and Employment*.

Roger Walden is Honorary Lecturer in Labour and Employment Law at Alliance Manchester Business School, Work and Equalities Institute University of Manchester. Roger is also a member of the Industrial Law Society and the Society of Legal Scholars.

Foreword

Winning workers more power, influence and voice at work has always been one of the trade union movement's defining causes. From the Tolpuddle Martyrs to digital campaigns to organise workers at Amazon and Uber, the story of trade unionism is about levelling the playing field for working people. This timely, important and thought-provoking book signposts how a new generation of labour activists can win workplace justice in a world that is changing fast.

Vividly illustrating the changes that are reshaping our working lives, the authors adopt a multidisciplinary approach that gives a broad and rich perspective of the realities facing workers today. Accessible and lively – and supported by a range of free resources – this book appeals beyond the usual academic audience to trade unionists, campaigners and activists. And its core message is that for all corporations and employers wield disproportionate clout, by acting collectively working people ourselves are powerful agents of change.

Disruptive change is nothing new. In the nineteenth century, the dark satanic mills of industrial Britain ushered in a new era of work intensity and exploitation – and underpinned the birth of the modern trade union movement. In the early twentieth century, Henry Ford's mass production lines gave an early taste of automation and mind-numbing alienation. And in the late twentieth century, the decline of manufacturing gave rise to the new service economy, emotional labour and new forms of casualisation.

What's different now, however, is the bewildering speed and scale of change. As the authors contend, globalisation, financialisation and new technology are radically reshaping capitalism. Global competition has uprooted entire industries. Tens of billions of pounds of investment can be shifted from one continent to another at the flick of a switch. And artificial intelligence and digitalisation are at the forefront of an information revolution even more transformative than its industrial counterpart. All of this fundamentally impacts on the relationship between capital and labour.

And these same forces are reshaping work itself. Insecurity, bogus self-employment and the gig economy are becoming the new normal. Millions of workers are now slaves to an app – at the beck and call of the boss any time, any place, anywhere. In contemporary Britain, one in nine workers is in precarious work, including a growing army of working people on zero-hours contracts and in sham self-employment. This is further distorting the balance of power in our labour market – and, as the book compellingly argues, the upshot is that work is being systematically decollectivised.

But all is not lost. Because while this brave new world undoubtedly presents huge challenges for workers and our unions, there are massive opportunities too. Amidst unprecedented digital disruption, industrial change and economic flux, it is still possible to fight fire with fire.

Perhaps most obviously, as the old adage goes, 'there is power in a union'. The book sets out how new forms of collective organisation, collective voice and social engagement can take root, not just providing checks and balances to global corporate power but contesting it. Even in today's fragmented and insecure labour market, collective action remains the best way for individuals to win work that is safe, secure and skilled, fairly rewarded and free from discrimination. What the late, great trade union leader Jack Jones said decades ago still holds true now: 'Organise, that's the magic word, because with organisation you can move mountains.'

And these new opportunities for labour mobilisation – innovative digital organising and campaign platforms targeting younger workers – can spark a wider trade union renewal. But while our destiny is ultimately in our hands, organised labour needs a new approach from government. As this book argues, a smart, active state can rebalance an employment relationship which has become dangerously skewed. More effective labour market regulation and stronger rights at work must be part of the policy mix. But ultimately, giving workers greater freedom to organise and union rights to bargain is our best way of building fairer, more equal workplaces. Rather than the draconian Trade Union Act, we need new laws to empower unions and workplace reps.

That's why the Trades Union Congress (TUC) recently used our 150th anniversary to call for a doubling of collective bargaining coverage. It's not just the best way to get wages rising and win fair shares for workers – the real wealth creators. It is also a powerful means with which to redistribute influence, voice and opportunity in our workplaces. Extreme inequality is ultimately unsustainable. Even the shock troops of global capital – the World Economic Forum, International Monetary Fund (IMF), Organisation for Economic Co-operation and Development (OECD) and *Financial Times* – are now calling for measures to boost the bargaining power of ordinary workers. Whether it's raising workers' living standards, greening the economy or avoiding another debt-driven financial crash, there is a growing consensus for change.

Those in the corridors of power could do worse than remember the famous words of Dr Martin Luther King: 'The labour movement did not diminish the strength of the nation but enlarged it. By raising the living standards of millions, labour miraculously created a market for industry and lifted the whole nation to undreamed of levels of production. Those who attack labour forget these simple truths, but history remembers them.'

Last but not least, more collective bargaining is also central to the success of the decent work agenda, across the world. From London to Lagos, it's only by banding together that workers can win better terms and conditions. And the authors chart how better jobs can become a reality – turning back the tide of casualisation and insecurity, and delivering the dignity workers deserve.

Power, politics and influence at work is a hugely valuable addition to the burgeoning debate about the future of work. And throughout, it stresses that workers and their unions are not passive observers, but the architects of our own future, sharing the benefits of new technologies to liberate working lives and make the market our servant, not our master.

What happens at work will shape the future of our economy, society and politics. A positive, progressive vision of better jobs, more collective bargaining and a strong voice for working people can put flesh on the bones of a new ideological settlement. Out of the rubble of neoliberalism must come something fairer, more equal and more sustainable. This book offers a route map towards the new deal to which working people are entitled.

Frances O'Grady

Frances O'Grady
TUC General Secretary

Abbreviations

ACAS	Advisory, Conciliation and Arbitration Service
CAC	Conciliation and Arbitration Committee
CIPD	Chartered Institute of Personnel and Development
CJEU	Court of Justice of the European Union
CSO	civil society organisation
DBEIS	Department for Business, Energy and Industrial Strategy
DBIS	Department for Business, Innovation and Skills
EAS	Employment Agency Standards Inspectorate
EAT	Employment Appeal Tribunal
EqA 2010	Equality Act 2010
ET	employment tribunal
EUWA	European Union (Withdrawal) Act 2018
HMRC	HM Revenue & Customs
HPWS	high-performance work systems
HRM	Human Resource Management

ICT	information communication technologies
IER	Institute of Employment Rights
ILO	International Labour Organization
IMF	International Monetary Fund
IWGB	Independent Workers' Union of Great Britain
JCC	joint consultative committee
LGBTQ+	lesbian, gay, bisexual, transgender and queer
NAECI	National Agreement for the Engineering Construction Industry
NGO	non-government organisation
NHS	National Health Service
NMW	National Minimum Wage
NSFE	non-standard forms of employment
OECD	Organisation for Economic Co-operation and Development
SECs	Sectoral Employment Commissions
SER	standard employment relationship
TUC	Trades Union Congress
UVW	United Voices of the World
WES	work and employment studies
WTR	Working Time Regulations 1998

1
Work, power and politics

Introduction

Most people enjoy work: it brings economic sustenance, mental attainment, a sense of fulfilment along with many positive social and community connections. However many people become 'alienated' from work, which means they end up feeling separated, socially and emotionally, from others in society, usually because of the way they are treated while at work by their boss or company – whether that is teaching children at school, repairing computers, providing domestic care for the elderly, or delivering food as an independent contractor via a smart phone app. In short, the systems that govern and regulate our employment conditions can be exploitative and shaped by sources of power in which many people lack a voice. Indeed, despite being devalued for decades, because of the COVID-19 crisis it is now obvious and visible how much we all rely on front line workers (e.g. those in health care, delivery drivers, shop assistants), many of whom are low paid and lack a meaningful voice at work.

The book is purposely short and presents a debate of select employment issues and opportunities for labour activism. It is not a textbook in the technical description of the word, although it underpins learning across generalist and bespoke types of educational programmes. In its entirety, the book presents an agenda for labour activism and future learning about the dynamics of power, politics and influence in a workplace. The book covers aspects of labour market inequalities, globalisation, technology, labour law and the contexts shaping the future of work. There is a free complementary learning module to engage further with such debates, including several video

interviews and related content that readers may find interesting on
FutureLearn.[1]

The book is structured as follows. In the remainder of this introductory chapter, we outline three models of power and then define
the 'work and employment studies' (WES) approach adopted
throughout the book. In Chapter 2 we look at shifts to non-standard
forms of work, the power of technology along with the importance of context and history, in order to better understand issues
of power and politics at work. In Chapter 3 the power of the state
and forms of employment regulation are debated. Chapter 4 then
discusses worker voice, trade unions and other advocacy groups
that can promote worker influence. Chapter 5 presents three future
developments on work and employment, each of which may vary
depending on the trajectories of power resources and political contexts for worker and agency alliances.

Power, influence and politics at work

Power has been defined as the 'ability of an individual or group to
control their physical and social environment; and as part of this
process, the ability to influence the decisions which are and are not
taken by others' (Hyman, 1975: 26). Employment relationships are
highly politicised and so power can be exerted individually, or collectively, to advance or suppress particular interests directly or indirectly, and to shape the spaces in which employers make choices that
affect workers' lives.

For example, under investor capitalism the Chief Finance
Officer of a large corporation, sitting in a plush office in downtown
Manhattan or the penthouse suite of a huge skyscraper in Hong
Kong, can influence the working lives of millions of people. They
may decide to switch the location of their corporation's global
supply network from parts of Indonesia or Vietnam to lower-cost
regions of Africa, for instance. Thousands of workers may be laid off
in one part of the world, communities devastated, as multinational
enterprises compete in a race to the bottom (e.g. seeking out the
lowest labour costs they can find). These decisions are deeply connected to power, politics, influence and the ways in which workers
can mobilise to challenge these corporate choices.

By contrast, some companies may actively choose to enhance employment standards that raise social and economic wellbeing; for instance, through more progressive corporate responsibility such as improving wages, supporting freedom of association and collective bargaining, or by protecting health and safety conditions. Unilever, for instance, is considered by some to be a better type of employer to some extent: it pays the real living wage to its UK workforce and claims as an ambition to try to end insecure employment among its supplier firms in less developed countries (Wilshaw *et al.*, 2016). Others, however, approach work and employment differently. For example Foxconn is a multinational corporation that manufactures electronic components that feature in the products of many well-known brands, such as Apple or Samsung, employing over one million workers worldwide, many housed in dormitory factories. One of Foxconn's largest facilities in Shenzhen, China, which in 2010 employed almost 500,000 employees, has been blighted with employment issues: long hours with no overtime pay, health and safety incidents, and when several workers committed suicide the company's response was to install safety nets between buildings (Chan *et al.*, 2020). Unfortunately, such tragic stories are not isolated. The disaster at Rana Plaza in Bangladesh in 2013 is another example of how power and politics affects peoples' lives. The Rana Plaza building, which housed several well-known retail corporations, collapsed with the tragic death of 1,134 garment workers. Part of the fallout of the disaster was a new voluntarist Accord that included union and worker representation as a form of private self-regulation, aimed at avoiding future tragedies (Donaghey and Reinecke, 2017). However, the fragility of such voluntary regulation is evidenced by the unilateral decision of the Bangladesh government to exclude the Accord from the country and thereby weaken labour protections, despite objections from trade unions and bodies such as the International Labour Organization (ILO). The rationale of the government was premised on the political desire for greater market liberalisation by removing any regulations that may add costs to protect workers. So, rather than systematically promoting better health and safety standards, the government opted for less protection for workers, commenting on the 'self-respecting nature' of regulation and arguing that 'there is no room for the Accord' (Safi, 2018).

This book aims to build activism and contribute to debates about the political character of power relations and employee influence in the workplace. It also considers how these issues connect to wider societal inequalities, as well as the role of the state and legal regulation in governing workplace relations Three useful conceptual frameworks which can assist in capturing the character of employment relations power are outlined next from French and Raven (1959), Lukes (1974, 2005) and Doellgast *et al.* (2018).

The six bases of power

French and Raven (1959) identified six bases of power underpinning social relationships (see Figure 1.1), which can also be viewed as different types of power that may be observed in different work situations. First, power is wielded through 'coercion', which may include a manager issuing a threat or a punishment to influence the actions of workers. Coercion can be emotional, political or physical and can manifest in relationships between workers and their managers. Second, individuals exercise power through their capacity to bestow

Figure 1.1 Bases of power

or restrict individual rewards (economic, social or emotional), such as a pay rise or promotion in a job. Third, power can be exerted due to individual 'expertise', including knowledge, skill or experience. Power is closely linked to 'legitimacy' which serves as French and Raven's (1959) fourth base of power. For example, certain social or cultural norms mean managers exercise power (real or presumed) to 'reward', 'punish' and 'manage' employees because of their position of authority within the organisational hierarchy.

French and Raven's (1959) fifth base of power is known as 'referent' power. It concerns how individuals exert power by securing respect from others. In such cases, individuals may serve as a 'role model', for example a union activist who is willing to stand up and defend the rights of others. French and Raven's (1959) sixth and final base of power is labelled 'informational', and refers to how individuals wield power based on the information or knowledge they possess. The latter form of power is perhaps increasingly salient today, because of advances in technology and artificial intelligence as ways to control data and manipulate the sources of information people can access.

French and Raven provide a useful starting point for identifying the way social relationships and interactions occur and evolve. Other frameworks of power seek to explain related facets of influence; in particular, how power may not always be immediately observable but can be used to shape an agenda or certain employment issues that favour one group over another.

The three faces of power

Lukes' (1974, 2005) framework may be seen to go further than that of French and Raven (1959), as it considers the different ways in which agendas are set and the approaches actors can take to leverage influence. This was achieved through the identification of 'three faces of power'. The first face of power evokes the work of Dahl (1957) and echoes to some extent the first power type in French and Raven's (1959) model: that of coercive actions. Lukes' (2005) first face of power concerns *observable* forms of domination. This assumes power is exerted when A influences B to do something he/she would not otherwise have done. For example, employers may have the capacity to implement organisational restructuring given their financial resources, including the offer of voluntary severance payments to employees, who may feel little alternative but to accept redundancy when confronted with how an employer can mobilise power resources of persuasion. Another example may involve employers exerting power on zero-hours workers, who may feel coerced to work all shifts offered to them because they can easily be replaced, especially when unemployment levels are high.

The second face of power is anchored in work by Bachrach and Baratz (1970) and pivots around the concept of 'non-decision making power', or agenda-setting. This face concerns how power is mobilised towards certain interests (managers), while curbing the alternative or opposing ideas of others (workers). For example, certain issues may be omitted from the agenda of a meeting by managers, thereby limiting the scope of workers or their union to influence a decision. In this way, Lukes shows how the potential for employees to exert influence can be restricted by boundaries set by management. Therefore, the full range of options are never fully known by workers or their representatives when management control the agenda for consultation.

Lukes' (1974, 2005) third and final face of power deals with subtle, latent or unobservable facets of influence, exerted through the manipulation of preferences. This third face of power concerns ideology, whereby individuals or groups may secure or maintain a position of dominance in order to advance their own interests. By manipulating ideas and preferences, particular actions and power relations are presented as 'common sense' or somehow seen as a 'natural' state of affairs. For example, certain job tasks may be done in certain and very specific ways because a practice has become embedded over time as a cultural norm. Accordingly, Lukes' (1974, 2005) framework highlights how particular agendas emerge and are controlled in workplace settings and presented as some sort of a *fait accompli*.

Despite the insights from Lukes' (2005) three faces of power, there are points of disagreement. For example, Lukes' (2005) third face has been criticised for prioritising '*power-over*', while side-stepping the notion of '*power-to*' (Edwards, 2006). The former refers to domination; a zero–sum concept where one individual or group is disadvantaged while another individual or group benefits at the former's expense. In contrast, '*power-to*' is a positive sum concept, where power exertion advances common interests that helps to 'get things done' in a more collaborative way (Sisson, 2012: 177). Power here can be productive and can leverage change to support or improve the conditions of workers. For example, managers may build power-sharing collaborations with employees, recognise and involve trade unions in decision-making outcomes, thereby supporting all parties to achieve desired goals, even when interests diverge or differ. Of course, such possibilities assume that managers are willing to share power in the first place, and that is never certain. Indeed, because of these points of debate, another approach from Doellgast *et al.* (2018) directs attention to issues affecting collective worker power in the broader regulatory context.

Reconstructing power solidarities

The third framework that will be used to position the political, social and institutional power relationships in work and employment is derived from Doellgast *et al.* (2018). This includes two discernible 'ideal type' models (see Figures 1.2 and 1.3), each having four interlinked conditions moulding the relative balance of power between employers, workers and their unions. These four conditions refer to 'institutions', 'employer strategies', 'union strategies' and 'worker identification'. Central to the framework is how representative structures differ and how they interact with welfare policies, labour market conditions and broader social context issues (unemployment, benefits, skills, education, social class and ethnicity, among others). The key issue here is that work-related strategies and practices must be understood in terms of the broader regulatory and socio-economic context. These are illustrated in the central column of boxes in Figures 1.2 and 1.3. The models are based on the notion that we need to extend our primary focus on the workplace unit and understand how worker influence develops in the broader context of socio-economic change, including how labour forms collective identities of their own.

The first model in Figure 1.2 defines a 'virtuous circle' of power with stable employment and strong regulations and policies. In this context, 'institutions' are inclusive as welfare supports, legislation and collective agreements cover a multitude of (standard and

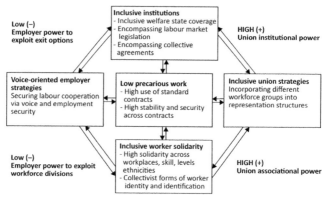

Source: Doellgast et al. (2018: 13)

Figure 1.2 A virtuous circle of solidarity

non-standard) working arrangements. Worker solidarity is identified; hence, workers can be motivated to take industrial action
and engage in collective co-operation with other workers who may
be in more disadvantaged positions than themselves, in terms of
their employment contract, pay and working conditions. Thus,
inclusive institutions support solidarities and associational union
power, which in turn promotes inclusive union representation
strategies. Furthermore, when institutions and solidarity are inclusive, employer power is constrained, which may stimulate voice-
orientated 'employer strategies' that enable greater worker capacity
for influence.

The second variation of the model (see Figure 1.3) defines a
'vicious circle' of power and influence where work is precarious, insecure and unstable. Under the contexts depicted in Figure 1.3, 'institutions' are fragmented and employment protections are weaker.
As a result employers exercise greater power to unilaterally impose
exit-orientated 'strategies' that push workers out of work, and/or
fuel 'exclusive union strategies', where unions are pressurised to prioritise the concerns of a select insider-group of members (e.g. core
workers) focused on standard employment contracts, while workers
under more precarious employment conditions are omitted as an
outsider-group. These very selective or exclusive union strategies,

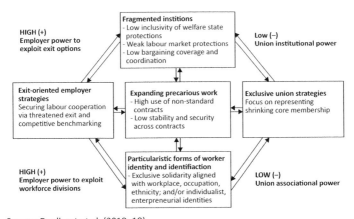

Source: Doellgast et al. (2018: 18)

Figure 1.3 A vicious circle of solidarity

when combined with employer attempts to divide the workforce, tend to fragment and weaken the possibilities for more power-based solidarities of 'worker identification'. For instance, workers may only identify and engage in collective solidarities with colleagues of the same skill level, functional role or ethnic background as themselves.

The value of Doellgast *et al.*'s (2018) framework is that it enables a consideration of micro, meso and macro contexts when analysing power, politics and influence in a workplace. Specifically, both models capture how regulatory systems and institutional processes intertwine with social actor agency capacity to foment competing contexts that support, or constrain, worker power and influence.

In taking the knowledge of different power frameworks further, we next outline WES as a distinct multidisciplinary field of study,[2] primarily integrating industrial relations, labour process theory, work sociology, law and heterodox economics and political science.

Work and employment studies: the 'indeterminacy' of labour power

The study of work and employment considers issues about, among other things, globalisation and capitalism, management actions vis-à-vis the utilisation of employees, worker voice, social class along with the institutions that regulate employment standards in different parts of the world. In this book we define WES as an approach that is multidisciplinary, drawing on the knowledge base of heterodox economics, radical law, industrial relations, critical psychology, sociology of work (particularly the labour process tradition) and historical and political approaches that affect power dynamics. Although workers' effort may possess the characteristics of a commodity in a narrow sense, in that it encompasses value and is traded in a labour market, it cannot be treated and analysed as a commodity because of its human dimension: it is embodied in the social and psychological character of people (Burawoy, 2013; Polanyi, 1957). WES perspectives draw from a critical social science tradition in that employers buy units of labour power – physical, mental and emotional effort – which includes workers' time. Worker effort (e.g. labour power) is variable and discretionary, meaning that few elements of the employment relationship can be stipulated in advance as the employer has to engage in various ways in order to utilise labour power in a productive but also co-operative manner, as Marx (1932) states in *Capital* (Volume I, chapters 6, 7 and 19). To this end, an important concept in understanding power and influence in employment is the nature of labour 'indeterminacy' (Baldamus, 1961; Kaufman and Gall, 2015; Laaser, 2010).

Labour indeterminacy is a concept to unpack some of the unequal power features of the employment relationship. It captures a permanent undercurrent of potential antipathy and tension between workers and managers, labelled as a 'structured antagonism' in the relations between worker and manager (Edwards, 1986). While a degree of mutual dependence exists between employers and employees, it is employers (and their managers acting on behalf of owners) who hold a power advantage in determining the terms and conditions of work within a specific regulatory context (Martínez Lucio and MacKenzie, 2017). Employers and workers often pursue potentially conflicting interests over how rewards are apportioned between profits and wages. This means that employment relationships are politically constructed (Kaufman and Barry, 2014) and that employers may utilise their inherent power advantage to craft governance systems that fulfil corporate, but not necessarily worker, interests (Dobbins *et al.*, 2017).

As a field of study WES contends that labour indeterminacy, combined with structural power imbalances and the mix of both co-operation and potential conflict, underscores an ongoing negotiated order, which in practice can be formal and/or informal (Baldamus, 1961). That is to say, the buying and selling of labour power is not, in the real world, the same as buying a chocolate bar or selling a car: rather it involves power, politics and forces of influence. Many such forces exist in the wider political, economic and social world beyond the immediacy of the workplace. Yet, organisational practices also have a degree of functional or 'relative' autonomy from external pressures, in the sense that changes in the wider political and economic world will not always impact directly on employment conditions (Thompson and Vincent, 2010). For example, wage rates are bound by market forces to some extent, but also determined by management choices and these choices can, in turn, be constrained by collective worker (union) solidarities that mitigate the effects of employer power, albeit in different ways (Martínez Lucio *et al.*, 2017). Researchers from WES traditions, broadly defined, seek to ameliorate the negative effects of power bias and safeguard labour and society. In order to understand these safeguards or interventions, a focus of study is on the institutions of governance and regulation, including trade unions and the nation state and how these may inject a more humane ethical value into the employment relationship (Kaufman and Barry, 2014). As you might expect, there are limits to these interventions to redress power imbalances, especially in the current economic context where institutions are being pushed towards ever-increasing corporate goals and private interests – including public and social organisations engaged with research and policy (Stewart and Martínez Lucio, 2017). What is more, the autonomy of institutions that have been created to balance relations between workers and their organisations are becoming themselves undermined and fragmented in the current economic context, as Chapter 2 will discuss.

WES perspectives often engage with public policy agendas and objectives for wider societal inclusion. Budd (2004) articulates such a goal in searching for a balance around competing objectives of 'efficiency', 'voice' and 'equality' in the workplace. The 'efficiency' component reflects employer burdens for increasing profit, along with higher wage demands from workers. However, as Budd (2004) argues, other dynamic features also exist, such as expectations for worker 'voice' and greater 'equality' in employment relationships (see Figure 1.4). The efficiency feature is premised on market rationality and *economic* perspectives, while ideas for worker 'voice' draw on *regulatory* and *institutional perspectives*. At the same time, *sociological* claims for decent work and human dignity call for greater 'equity' at work than the market rationality approach alone can achieve. Combined, the 'efficiency–equity–voice' framework resonates with the inclusive and multidisciplinary dimensions of WES as an approach to study labour market phenomena and employment issues. According to Budd's perspective, positions of the triad (Figure 1.4) may signal unstable and unequal power relationships, and the goal is to achieve a balance across all three positions in support of a social contract and better democratic compromise at the very least.

One way to capture the interplay of politics, power and influence between these simultaneous competing facets of efficiency, voice and equality are underlying 'frames of reference' (Budd and Zagelmeyer, 2010; Dobbins and Dundon, 2017; Fox, 1966; Heery, 2016). First is a 'unitarist' frame, which would rationalise management choice around a presumed set of shared interests between workers and employers. The assumption is that managers have the 'right to manage' without

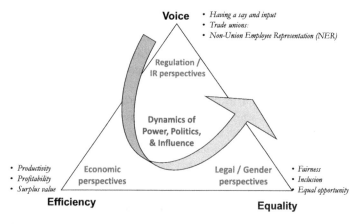

Figure 1.4 Efficiency, equity and voice framework

external third party intervention (for example unions or a regulatory state) and where direct communication between managers and employees is seen as the best way of creating a corporate culture and achieving common goals. Historically, this would have been the main frame of reference within the nineteenth century during the emergence of more systematic and hierarchical management systems. A variant of unitarism is what Budd (2004) describes as the '*egoist*', who views the employment relationship as an extension of free market principles. Although exceptions may be noted in the form of some 'enlightened' and socially oriented unitarist employers (examples include Cadbury's or Unilever based on Quaker values), these companies often denied collective worker representation as trade unions were regarded as an interference into the market (egoist) and management's unilateral right to manage (unitarist).

The twentieth century saw the steady evolution of another frame of reference, that of 'pluralism', which favoured choices that might permit joint consultation and participation in decision-making, echoed in tripartite governance structures found in global institutions such as the ILO and Bretton Woods arrangement for consensus development. A post-Second World War consensus system which ran until 1980 was seen as a pluralist watershed in the UK and Western Europe at that time, as was the New Deal period in the United States. Under pluralist approaches, a strengthening of worker input into managerial decisions provided a degree of power-sharing in the alignments between 'efficiency, equity and voice' (Budd, 2004; Kochan and Osterman, 1994). Pluralists infer that a weakening of worker power may in fact contribute to an economic shift towards low-quality jobs that have negative societal spill-over effects (Nolan and Marginson, 1990).

The final frame of reference is a 'radical' (or critical) view, which places less emphasis on shared goals between the parties (unitarist) or the institutional reforms for better joint regulation (pluralist), that in many of its approaches highlights the tensions that evolve from an employment relation based on capitalist ownership of the means of production (Hyman, 1975). Instead, the radical frame stresses how the shifts in capitalism, along with changing political values, have hollowed-out worker and trade union capabilities to influence the sources of power in a workplace (Heery, 2016; Kelly, 2011). The radical perspective argues that there are limits to the way a political consensus can emerge between labour and capital in the current socio-economic context, such that it is always contingent and never fully embedded given the nature of power asymmetries.

Overall, the concepts of labour indeterminacy, structured antagonism and the challenges to balancing efficiency–equity–voice point to six overlapping dimensions that capture the power and political dynamics of WES as a distinct approach, building on Martínez Lucio (2006, 2016b). These six dimensions are developed and summarised in Table 1.1 and teased out in the discussions in subsequent chapters of the book.

Building on the definitions of WES in this chapter, issues arising from globalisation, labour market re-structuring and outsourcing – as well as technological changes – that has expanded precarious work and new technologies are debated in Chapter 2. The importance of history and the legacy effects of context are reviewed, and the challenges for workers and unions from the likes of digital labour platforms and diminished job tenure are also considered. Chapter 2 emphasises how different factors intertwine and contribute to an ongoing level of fragmentation at work.

Chapter 3 then maps out how the nation state (government) influences employment conditions. It emphasises that an ongoing decollectivisation and de-regulation of work through the individualisation of employment rights has weakened the power of organised labour. It discusses new work arrangements such as the gig economy, resulting in bogus self-employment, showing how state institutions and the judiciary have contributed to further inequalities regardless of their formal or rhetorical commitments to equality broadly speaking.

Chapter 4 then discusses who speaks for whom at work. It charts the power and equitable effects of collective bargaining, issues of non-union employee voice mechanisms, and social dialogue opportunities from new network-based civil society alliances and networks beyond the workplace. It attempts to map worker representation and how it is evolving across various fronts leading to a more complex system of labour relations based on ongoing change and alliances and tensions between a broader range of organisations.

Chapter 5 provides the conclusion. It summarises the argument that while work and employment relationships are increasingly fragmented and disjointed, with diminished power and influence for

Table 1.1 Structure of the book

Dimension of work and employment power and politics	Relevant chapters
Labour indeterminacy and structured antagonism	The workplace as a unit of analysis; sources of power and solidarity; managerial framing; selection, consent and resistance; work and employment as a field of study are all introduced in Chapter 1
Management actions, labour market utilisation and new technologies	New forms of worker utilisation and motivation; history and legacy effects on work behaviours; labour market fragmentation; precarious work; new technology and work are discussed in Chapter 2
The global dimension	Globalisation and increased spatial mobility of employment, including shift to financialised capitalism, are also covered in Chapter 2
The state and employment regulation	The evolving roles of the nation state; employment laws and political discourse of regulation; gender and inequalities are discussed in Chapter 3
The communication sphere	Social dialogue, collective bargaining, employer tactics to avoid unions, community co-operatives and the institutions of worker voice are outlined and debated in Chapter 4
The future of work contexts	Multiple future developments reviewing voice; fragmentation of power and influence; minimalist state interventions; reformulated collective mobilisations along with new patterns of network alliance-building among unions and community activist groups are discussed in Chapter 5

Source: Developed and modified from Martínez Lucio (2016b: 19).

many workers, there are optimistic features and the capacity for collective and network alliance-building can mobilise positive change in the future. Chapter 5 briefly outlines a range of positive and negative potential outcomes but three broad futuristic developments at work are outlined which vary in emphasis. None of these are intentionally deterministic or static, and each presents multiple trajectories of influence, subject to the interplay of various forces and power resources discussed in the book. It is important for worker organisations and activists to reflect on the complexity of new and evolving diverse spaces that can challenge inequalities and support worker voice. Some of the challenges include finding ways to create social and political alliances and strategies that ensure a greater degree of fairness, purpose and meaning within work and society.

Conclusion

This introductory chapter has outlined three models of power: 'six bases' of power; 'three faces' of power; and 'collective power solidarities'. It then defined WES as a field of study, building on six dimensions incorporating: (1) labour indeterminacy and frames of reference; (2) managerial actions concerning worker utilisation and market forces; (3) globalisation; (4) the role of the state and employment regulation; (5) the communicative sphere for worker voice; and (6) the contexts for variable work futures and developments. These dimensions are the basis for how the argument in the book evolves from the context of labour market and workplace change, in terms of globalisation and technology, through to a discussion of the changing regulatory context and then finally focusing on the way worker voice and representation is shifting and becoming more fragmented in some ways but more flexible and dexterous politically in others. It is hoped the book will be a resource for related online learning and labour activism, with added content including video interviews with leading scholars whose research is referenced in the book, plus various labour activists and policy advocates promoting better regulation and a more equitable and sustainable work future.

Notes

1 www.futurelearn.com/courses/work-power-politics-influence.
2 WES here is a description for a broad field of study, different to the aims of an academic journal of the same acronym, *Work, Employment & Society*. As a field of study WES is multidisciplinary, including industrial relations, sociology, psychology, history, law and labour economics (among others).

2
History, global capitalism and contexts

Introduction

This chapter discusses the various socio–economic developments that have created the political climate that shapes the balance of power between employers and employees. The next section reviews briefly the importance of history, outlining the organising and dis-organising of industrial capitalism and the implications for power, politics and influence in employment. Next, three significant themes are discussed that have led to shifts in the nature of work and eroded the foundations for greater influence: *globalisation*, *financialisation* and *technological change*. The themes have consequences that affect the fragmentation of power, politics and influence that connect to debates in Chapter 3 (the state and legal regulation) and Chapter 4 (worker and union voices) that have eroded what many call the standard employment relationship (SER). Accordingly, there is an increasing threat from the rise in non-standard forms of employment (NSFE) with growing numbers of workers engaged in temporary, part-time and subcontractual arrangements. This is illustrated in the following section with references to platform work, a contemporary form of employment that symbolises many of the characteristics of NSFE. Finally, the chapter concludes by considering debates concerning the future of work, specifically the claims that automation will lead to the demise of work as we know it. This chapter shows how, over time, there is an erosion of worker power, although options for newer, reinvigorated patterns of influence are further picked up in subsequent chapters.

The organising and disorganising nature of contemporary capitalism

The historical trajectory of employment since the twentieth century shows highly cyclical patterns of influence, with a waxing and waning of power – from dependency on agricultural work, the expansion of cottage industries, industrialisation and the rise of bureaucracy, to contemporary debates about union decline, globalisation, financialisation and the rise of the gig economy, as discussed later in this chapter. It is important to view these changes in a historical context, in order to evaluate and understand the nature of the changes taking place in terms of worker voice.

There is an argument that, during the mid- to late twentieth century, especially in developed countries, we saw a more organised and centralised system of labour and employment relations that allowed trade unionists and collective worker representatives to influence the nature of their working environments and the way they were rewarded through pay and the social services of the state (Lash and Urry, 1987). This was a moment of extensive coordination within the regulation of work and employment, with certain national contexts seeing more extensive worker political influence (Hall and Soskice, 2001). There have been questions about the extent of this influence and the partially mythical status it has taken on; however, various characteristics of Fordist and industrialised – and organised – capitalism supported trade unions, becoming significant players in the area of labour regulation, especially in developed countries.

First, during industrialised capitalism the scale of the workplace usually became larger and there was a greater concentration of workers, allowing for economies of scale in terms of the organising of trade union structures. The nature of Fordism and industrial organisation was not necessarily beneficial for workers, due to de-skilling, but it did allow them to organise themselves and constrain management prerogative by virtue of the sheer concentration of employment processes. The organisation of the employment relation in terms of performance management and controls systems did, ironically, establish a clearer basis for negotiating payment and reward systems. The relative certainty and predictability within employment relations thus allowed for a degree of structured regulation and worker involvement on specific work and employment issues (Lipietz, 1997).

Second, the extensive level of economic growth and the relatively more secure nature of the firm during the 1940s through to the 1980s (approximately) allowed for greater concessions to workers and more extensive forms of collective bargaining to flourish, both formally and informally, between workers and their managers. The fact that capital remained relatively immobile at this stage meant that there were clear lines of external and inward investment, which during the second half of the twentieth century did not undermine the basic structure of national economies, especially in more developed geographies, and thus concessions from capital were possible with growth and settled national contexts.

Third, the political influence of organised labour, through their allied social democratic and broader left-wing parties, especially in the West European context, further facilitated a degree of political influence within the state and led to more social orientation; for example, in the form of extensive welfare service provision. The importance of organised labour to national political discourse was steadily emerging prior to the Second World War as unions established a greater presence strategically and structurally in the realm of the political (Marks, 2014). These factors are not to suggest that that there was a clear and consistent moment of unity and ideological uniformity within the workforce, and that the influence of trade unions extended towards all the different segments of the labour market. There were strong hierarchies within the labour market in terms of gender and ethnicity, for example, with regard to varying levels of pay, segregation and exclusion at work, and general questions of fairness (Rubery and Hebson, 2018). With respect to immigrants, trade unions were not consistently supportive of their needs, although this has been steadily changing (Fine and Tichenor, 2009). In this respect, even during organised and more stable moments of capitalism (organised capitalism) there were points of exclusion and segmentation in relation to some groups of workers.

The political, social and economic contexts of labour and employment relations – which are at the heart of how we approach work and employment relations in this text – are therefore important in framing the way issues of representation are configured and how

they change. They may be part of a general set of developments that
permit workers a greater influence and role within society, and the
firm in some cases, although there is a general understanding that
developments since the early 1980s have created a more hostile and
challenging environment for organised labour and collective worker
participation. For example, where once employers may have seen
the logic of sustaining and supporting organised labour in order to
create a more coordinated form of job regulation and avoid industrial conflict, increasingly employers endeavour to restrain or limit
'collectiveness' among employees. This has been done through the
development of new forms of collective representation that have
tended to be employer–dominated rather than employee-led, often
featuring the use of teamwork and, in some cases, replacing or dis-
abling unions with direct management-led communication systems
and processes (McBride and Martínez Lucio, 2011; see Garrahan
and Stewart, 1992; Storey and Bacon, 1993, for earlier interventions). Statistics illustrate a decline in trade union representation
since the early 1980s in many developed economies (Kochan *et al.*,
1986; Van Wanrooy *et al.*, 2013). The percentage of workers able
to harness collective agreements as a vehicle to leverage influence
on issues such as pay or working time has decreased significantly
in cases such as the UK, notably in the private sector, although a
substantial minority of the workforce still have the terms and conditions of their employment determined by collective bargaining.
There is also increased reliance on minimum wage legislation
and greater orientation of low-paid work towards that minimum
(Rubery *et al.*, 2016). The use of such a minimum wage system can
sometimes allow employers – especially small and medium-sized
employers – to link their payment systems and avoid higher-level
wage agreements.

The sharp decrease in the use of industrial action as a source
of worker and collective influence exemplifies changing capacities
and shifts in the balance of power. Alongside diminished collective
power and worker mobilisation, in the UK, for example, the state
increasingly enforces significant restrictions on strike action (e.g.
the 2016 Trade Union Act which sets certain thresholds in the vot-
ing turnout for strike ballots). However, declining strike action may
not, in itself, signal an absence of conflict, and options for employee

influence may be seen in extended absenteeism or other forms of individual dissent (Edwards, 1995; Van den Broek and Dundon, 2012). These issues will be discussed further in Chapter 4.

There is also a set of developments within the labour market (discussed below) that point to the way employers exploit divisions within the workforce in terms of age, race, sex or religion (Heery, 2016) and constrain or limit worker voice (Doussard, 2013). Working arrangements such as part-time work, casualisation, individual payment systems or different employment contract status also impair a worker's capacity to influence decisions in the workplace. That is not to say that alternative forms of collective solidarity cannot emerge between these new social groups in terms of union organisation, action and strategy (Connolly *et al.*, 2014a); however, there is a growing level of social fragmentation that can run alongside – and be accelerated by – the political climate of greater de-regulation in labour and employment relations as illustrated below. Current studies also emphasise the fundamental shift towards a more flexible and decentralised economy and labour market (Carter *et al.*, 2011) as we will outline below. The global level focus on cost-efficiency, competition and the managerial use of the customer paradigm constitute prominent underlying catalysts of change (Martínez Lucio, 2016a). Heightening flexibilisation, precarious work (including agency, part-time, subcontracting, temporary) and new forms of information communication technologies (ICTs) have created a greater spatial and labour market dispersion of the workforce with new forms of employers exploiting this dispersion more directly (Howcroft and Taylor, 2014; Weil, 2014). Such developments have longer-term social and personal implications creating an ever more *insecure* culture within working lives (Sennett, 1998). These changes have paralleled the development of a political environment since the 1980s that weakens the influence of organised workers (Howell, 2005; Streeck, 2011) as Chapter 3 will outline.

Increasing market forces are playing a prominent role in shaping the balance of power in employment relationships, e.g. the strategic use by management of unemployment and forms of flexibility at work. Other salient factors affecting the balance of power may be micro-oriented, say in relation to specific employee skills demanded by an employer, such as certain technological job competencies.

However, while there are incidences of particular skills and expertise leveraging individual power, such generalities are limited in the job market and a more realistic evaluation is that most employers can access a relatively large pool of workers (Holmes and Mayhew, 2012; Lansley, 2011).

More structural aspects define the position of workers in the labour market. Recent decades have seen a downward trend in the labour income share across both advanced and developing economies (IMF, 2017a). For example, one study found that between 1990 and 2009 the share of labour compensation in national income declined in 26 out of 30 advanced countries and the median (adjusted) labour share of national income across these countries fell from 66.1 to 61.7 per cent (ILO and OECD, 2015). The US economy in particular is renowned for long-term wage stagnation: in 2017 real wages were only 10 per cent higher than those in 1973 (Shambaugh *et al.*, 2017). The picture is similar for the UK, which stands out as the only advanced economy where wages contracted between 2007 and 2016 despite economic growth. In 2014 UK real wages were almost 10 per cent lower than before the 2008 crisis, while those in France and Germany had grown by 7 per cent (Romei, 2017). Machin and Costa (2017) have shown how 'almost all groups of individuals and families – with the exception of minimum wage workers and pensioners – are no better off on average than they were in 2008'. Self-employed individuals have been particularly affected with median real weekly incomes almost 20 per cent lower.

Globalisation, financialisation and technological change

Changing dynamics, which include globalisation, financialisation and technological change, have led to shifts in the nature of employment. These contextual influences shape labour markets, the availability of jobs, worker mobility and skills demands, and illustrate how power relations between employers and employees are situated within broader shifts in contemporary capitalism. In the main, developments along these three contextual factors have eroded the environment that sustained a stronger and collective worker voice.

The globalisation of capitalism

The globalisation of capitalism is one of the main disorganising factors in relation to how work and employment is influenced and shaped. In some sense the concept of globalisation should have been a development that enhances work and employment as countries converge in terms of their employment practices, management structures and systems of worker rights. There has been much optimism about the fact that we are seeing greater trade flow between nations and that organisations are creating bridges across what were once isolated or separate parts of the globe. On the right of the political spectrum there are those who see globalisation in a positive light with the opening of product and labour markets: a critical step to a greater exchange of ideas, practices and cultures through the role of the market. These belong to a more neoclassical market-oriented view of social and political development. Friedman, for example, in the *World is Flat* (2005), sees the current age as one based on free market capitalism which in turn hinges on a process of extensive Americanisation in terms of how countries are regulating their economies. The idea of greater 'democratisation' emerging from such influences is central to this thesis, as can be seen in Wolf's *Why Globalization Works* (2004) which sees the liberal market as a 'good thing' for workers and businesses.

However, the main debates on globalisation are often sanguine or even critical, not because greater convergence between countries is seen as a 'bad thing' but quite the contrary. The issue concerns *how* convergence is taking place and the way, ironically, it is undermining the social and employment rights of workers. For example, there is considerable evidence that the growing power of multinational corporations enables them to have an advantage over nation states as they can literally 'regime shop', looking for the cheapest labour, easier access to natural resources and less labour market rigidity as a way to bypass labour rights (Almond and González Menéndez, 2014). Governments are increasingly forced to constrain the costs of labour and workers' rights in an attempt to make their national sites more attractive to international capital (see Chapter 3). This has the effect of lowering social standards as governments generate greater interest in reducing labour regulation and rights whilst even creating 'special enterprise zones' which can suspend the body of worker rights so as to attract foreign investment.

Operationally, a manufacturing multinational has the ability to seek concessions from its workforce (e.g. lower wages, deterioration of working conditions etc.) by threatening to move to other locations and sites (Greer and Hauptmeier, 2016). The constant threat of disinvestment in seeking concessions from labour is a common practice among multinational corporations and generates vulnerability among workers. One must keep in mind that a quarter of the global economy is managed by multinational corporations (UNCTAD, 2011) and they have been known to deploy 'whipsawing' tactics; that is, playing groups of workers in different countries (and plants) against each other in the attempt to seek more 'compliant' production and service delivery practices from the point of view of management.

Dicken (2007) argued that multinational corporations take part in unequal exchange relationships with governments, social organisations and unions because the latter are fixed within specific spaces. There are winners and losers: but the latter are normally those on the periphery of the exchange network, such as children making clothes in parts of Asia or working in the cocoa industry in western Africa (Barrientos, 2001). Whilst the United States is not the main or sole driver of globalisation, the structure of the global economy remains significantly hierarchical even if new players such as China have entered the fray. Hirst and Thompson (1999) point out that global economic flows follow a specific course around privileged, dominant and more developed areas. Production and distribution remain unequally distributed and shared. Hence, the impact of globalisation from the perspective of workers is a mixed blessing as it brings employment to underdeveloped regions but also recreates new hierarchies, sustains older ones, limits the role of the state and generates pressures on workers to make concessions both materially and politically.

This power of mobility attributed to multinational corporations cannot be assumed given that multinationals are often reliant on national groups of workers for specific skills and national states for infrastructure – so there are limits (see Lillie and Martínez Lucio, 2012). Furthermore, there is a new emerging working class throughout the world which is more politicised in some respects due to these investment flows and strategies (Ness, 2016). Nevertheless, the balance of power between workers and management has tended to shift to the latter given the market and neoliberal underpinnings of globalisation as it is now currently structured and configured.

The financialisation of capitalism

Global financialisation is another related contextual factor that shapes work and employment relations. The rise in shareholder capitalism, with its focus on maximising shareholder value (Lazonick and O'Sullivan, 2000), and the subsequent process of financialisation, whereby profits are increasingly created through financial channels and investments rather than productive value-added services or activities, has enabled more volatile investments. It requires a flexibility which extends beyond 'operational' concerns to handle changes in demand and personnel through natural attrition and temporary absence through leave and has therefore had major implications for work and employment relationship dynamics (Thompson, 2013). The demand for short-term financial results necessitates adaptations which may well result in workers being laid off (Lazonick and O'Sullivan, 2000). It also informs a preference for individualistic performance-related pay systems, investments in general rather than firm-specific skills, and hostility towards union bargaining (Jacoby, 2005). Various strategies to maximise shareholder value, such as private equity buyouts and stock buybacks to manipulate stock price, have further weakened the position of employees (Appelbaum *et al.*, 2013). These strategies have informed business models that transfer economic risk to labour and increase insecurity (Findlay *et al.*, 2017). They also reduce labour's share of income and exert pressure on supply chains.

These processes have particularly affected what are termed liberal market economies, such as the United States and the United Kingdom, which are characterised by strong shareholder pressures, but have also extended to more stakeholder-oriented economies. It has affected the balance of power between capital and labour as illustrated by Thompson's (2003, 2013) Disconnected Capitalism Thesis, which refers to the growing divergent requirements of firms in terms of work and employment, 'between what capital is seeking from employees ... and what it finds necessary to enforce in the realm of employment relations' (Thompson, 2003: 364). On the one hand, demands on employees have increased in terms of effort, commitment and emotional engagement. Some reviews point to high-performance work systems (HPWS) that aim to promote employee engagement through progressive human resource management practices. However, others point out how the processes of financialisation have led to delayering, downsizing and divestment, as firms have retreated from investments in human capital and reduced the quality of employment in terms of security, career development and pensions. Even more striking has been the impact of financialisation on the fragmentation of employment as the drive to reduce costs and increase flexibility has forced an increasing share of workers out of stable employment with a single employer (Marchington *et al.*, 2005). The next section will discuss this development in greater detail.

The impact of technology and technological change

The impact of new technologies on employment relations has also played out in multifarious forms across organisations and sectors, uncovering context-specific multifaceted forces (Howcroft and Taylor, 2014). For many commentators, as increasing numbers of people shift from agricultural and manufacturing labour to service work, visions of a 'knowledge economy' and the emergence of informational capitalism (Castells, 1996) are viewed through a positive lens. Without doubt, incremental advances have seen ICTs shape working practices in numerous ways, but crucially, the effects and consequences rarely play out as predicted. Digital technologies are designed and implemented under conditions where power resides with employers, not employees, and in circumstances where technological systems are developed to serve the interests of capitalist firms (Spencer, 2017). Sociotechnical change has led to the increasing displacement of certain occupations (e.g. bank cashiers, travel agents, switchboard operators etc.), while new types of jobs have been enabled by developments in ICTs (e.g. call centre agents). A major impact on working life has been the embedding of technology in working practices in order to monitor the productivity and performance of workers (Taylor and Bain, 1999, 2007). While managing performance is arguably the key concern of management, demands for greater accountability to consumers and citizens, particularly in the public sector, has meant that performance monitoring is increasingly ubiquitous and intensive. This is despite the lack of evidence which shows formalised performance management actually improves performance or productivity (Findlay and Thompson, 2017). History shows that technology can often be employed as a mechanism of control and to direct workflow rather than as a means to upskill workers and minimise 'grunt work'. This application of technology is evident across areas such as the bio-tracking of workers (previously used for animals), the use of sensors in the helmets of electricians and train drivers to detect fatigue and stress, and the wearing of digital wristbands by Amazon warehouse pickers which constantly track and rate productivity levels (see Bloodworth, 2018).

Fragmentation and flexibilisation at work

An additional element that has shaped power relations is employment fragmentation as more workers no longer have stable employment with a single employer (Marchington *et al.*, 2005). Two major developments can be distinguished in this respect. First, there has been a rise in NSFE, which concerns forms of work that fall outside the scope of the SER and refers to employees in temporary employment (fixed-term contracts, seasonal work, casual work), temporary agency work or other contractual arrangements that involve multiple parties and part-time employment (Rubery, 2005).[1] It can also include self-employed workers that depend on a single or a small number of clients. The increase in NSFE has informed concerns about the rising precariousness of employment. While some of these workers with higher skill or status may be in a relatively strong position to influence their employment conditions, they represent a minority. COVID-19 exemplifies the tragic implications of precarious contracts. When governments in several countries closed hospitality and leisure organisations (e.g. pubs, restaurants, cafes, gyms), temporary workers in these organisations and related organisations (e.g. taxi drivers), faced significant uncertainty around how they would make ends meet. Government support for temporary and self-employed workers during the COVID-19 crisis varied by country (TUC, 2020). A second source of fragmentation concerns the growth of outsourcing and subcontracting, both nationally and internationally, which has been facilitated by processes of globalisation and sociotechnical change. This has laid the foundation for the 'lifting and shifting' of work to lower-cost geographies, expanding offshoring and outsourcing to large segments of the service industry as capital searches for a new 'spatial fix' (Harvey, 2006). But it has also affected those jobs that remain locally. Many workers at supply firms may remain on standard employment contracts but the dependence on particular contracts and clients can enhance the precarity of this type of employment. It may limit employee capacity to influence working conditions given the short-term nature of many outsourcing contracts, limited investment in training and low levels of pay where contracts prioritise cost-minimisation (Grimshaw *et al.*, 2016). The challenges that employment fragmentation poses in terms of developing a motivated and productive workforce are obvious, and this is underlined by research that shows that employment flexibility negatively interacts with innovation and productivity (Rubery *et al.*, 2016).

The flexibilisation of employment concerns 'how we work, under what forms of employment contract, for how many hours, at what times of day and with what degrees of employment security' (Rubery, 2015: 634). The concept gained momentum in the 1980s, during periods of severe unemployment and intense competition. Today, job market flexibility is an area riven with debate (Benassi, 2013; Grimshaw *et al.*, 2016; Keune and Serrano, 2014; Rubery *et al.*, 2016). Proponents of flexibilisation, often influenced by neoclassical economics, deem it crucial for cost-efficiency and eliminating job market blemishes. According to this perspective, employers expand their adoption of NSFE in order to increase flexibility and lower costs since it enables them to evade employment protection legislation and the (stronger) bargaining power of SER workers. However, the rise in flexibility cannot be separated from financialisation, which has raised the demand for flexibility beyond operational considerations and workforce planning. An important aspect of the debates concerns labour market segmentation between 'good' jobs, defined by standard employment relationships, and 'bad' jobs characterised by, for, example, variable hours (part-time employment), employment insecurity (fixed-term contracts, outsourced employment) or both (zero-hour and 'if and when' contracts) (O'Sullivan *et al.*, 2015). Crucially, 'labour market segmentation theory' (Craig *et al.*, 1982; Rubery, 1978) has long mapped how wider socio-political and economic forces divide the job market into distinct sub-groups, not only based on productivity and skills, but also discriminatorily by sex, race and age. The rise in NSFE has given poignancy to these theories with Emmenegger *et al.* (2012) referring to 'the age of dualisation' in Europe.

These developments are far from uniform and the data on the prevalence of NSFE and subcontracting show important differences between countries. Most countries have seen a rising trend concerning these employment types, although this has been affected by economic fortunes, with many temporary workers laid off after the 2008 crisis. Figure 2.1 shows the share of temporary employment in a number of European countries since 2007.[2] The data show important inter-country differences that illustrate how job markets can have very specific dynamics based on important differences in, for example, regulation and industries. There are several countries that show a consistently high share of temporary employment (i.e. Spain) and countries that have seen a strong rise in recent years (i.e. Netherlands, Croatia). However, the data also show that the share of temporary employment among both earlier (EU-15) and later

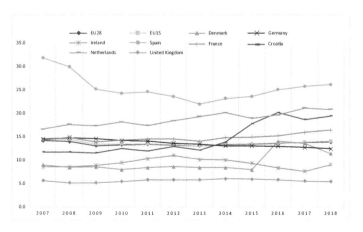

Figure 2.1 Temporary employees as a share of total employment, 2007–2018

(EU–28) member countries of the European Union has remained rather stable.

The picture changes somewhat when we consider other NSFE. Figure 2.2 shows the share of part-time employment in various European countries since 2007. There are important differences between countries. For example, the Netherlands is a clear outlier, reflecting the dominance of part-employment, particularly among women. The character of part-time employment can also differ substantially. As indicated by the rising share, part-time employment has in many ways become a new standard in the Netherlands and can no longer be considered 'non-regular' or 'atypical' (Plantenga, 2002; Visser, 2002). The process of 'regularisation' has extended to the character of part-time employment, resulting in an important equality with full-time employment in terms of wages, employment stability, social security, etc. This provides a relative contrast to the UK where much part-time employment continues to be characterised by low-level jobs and low earnings (Grimshaw *et al.*, 2016).

Another important development has been the rise in self-employment. In the UK this form of employment has seen the largest increase since the 2008 financial crisis, accounting for 45 per cent of growth (ONS, 2016). However, recent entrants to this category

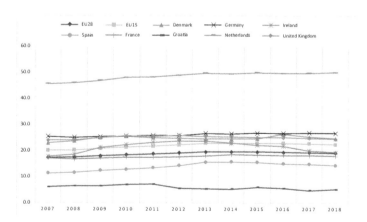

Figure 2.2 Part-time employment as a share of total employment, 2007–2018

contrast significantly with the conventional definition of the capitalist entrepreneur overseeing a large firm and are far more likely to be lone self-employed with no employees. In terms of occupational distribution, the newly emerging self-employed fall broadly into two tribes (The Resolution Foundation, 2017). On the one hand, there has been a significant rise in technical and professional roles associated with IT, design and engineering (this has increased by 27 per cent since 2011). These occupations are comparatively highly paid and so taxation benefits are seen as a key driver for growth in this category. The other category represents growth in precarious self-employed, those whose position is structurally insecure and who are predominantly represented by the young, underemployed and poorly paid. One explanation for its increase is that as austerity takes hold, people are 'pushed' into self-employment as a source of livelihood with growth more accurately categorised as 'involuntary self-employment' (Kautonen *et al.*, 2010). Numerous lawsuits reveal that many people within the category of precarious self-employment fall under 'bogus self-employment', whereby this employment type is seen as a euphemism for 'regular' work whereby the employee is unprotected by minimum wage legislation or other workplace entitlements (see also Chapter 3). Given the negligible levels of autonomy and highly formalised labour process, workers enjoy none of the benefits of self-employment, while bearing all the costs (e.g. no sickness cover and pensions). Employers who are sourcing labour via the self-employed category reap the benefits of significant tax savings as well as numerical flexibility. While workers in the gig economy have tended to dominate the debate about bogus self-employed, this category also includes other types of occupations such as construction workers (Behling and Harvey, 2015) and sex workers (Cruz *et al.*, 2017).

The rise in NSFE is obvious, but one could question whether it is as significant as the intensity of the debate on fragmentation and precariousness would suggest. In several countries the percentages appear remarkably stable. This also appears to be the case when we focus on developments in the UK (Figure 2.3). Part-time and temporary employment has been fairly stable while the rise in self-employment and zero-hours contracts may appear less significant than publicity suggests. This can be partly explained by the relative

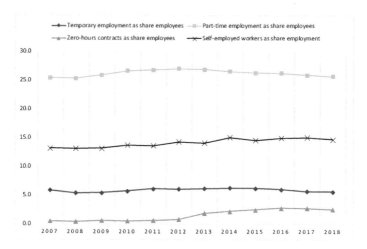

Figure 2.3 NSFE as a share of total employment UK, 2007–2018

loose regulation for permanent employment contracts. For example, the right to claim unfair dismissal requires a minimum of two
years' continuous service and this has reduced the perceived need
for fixed-term contracts.

However, the data also tend to underestimate the significance of
the developments. Overall, the majority of jobs created since the
2008 financial crisis have concerned part-time employment, zero-
hours contracts and self-employment (Rubery *et al.*, 2016). This has
been considered a major factor behind the fall in UK real wages
(Machin and Costa, 2017; Romei, 2017), suggesting the crisis has
accelerated the rise in NSFE. For example, the share of zero-hours
contracts in the UK increased almost fivefold between 2011 and
2016 from 0.6 to 2.8 per cent of all employees. Moreover, statistical
ambiguities obscure the precarious character of much employment,
as evidenced by employment in the UK care sector. National data
for 2016 show that 90 per cent of workers have a permanent contract, confirming the relative low share of temporary employment
in the UK. At the same time, 24 per cent of jobs constitute zero-
hours contracts, with 80 per cent of these workers on a permanent
zero-hours contract. If these workers are included among temporary employment, justified by the lack of any guarantees in terms of

employment continuity and hours, its share rises to 27.9 per cent of total employment (Skills for Care, 2016). Furthermore, the impact of subcontracting and outsourcing is barely captured by national data, while there has been a major impact on activities such as catering, cleaning and care provision. For example, over 85 per cent of all employees in the adult care sector are not directly employed by local authorities or the National Health Service (NHS) and their employment is thus conditional on a specific contract (Skills for Care, 2016). These jobs are peculiarly shaped by the conditions of the outsourcing contract with job security hampered by the short-term nature of many outsourcing contracts and the risk of contract loss. Training and career development prospects may be also be impaired by a tendency for outsourced work to generate narrower, specialised job categories so that performance can be more clearly monitored between client and supplier organisations. Meanwhile, pay may be constrained by the strong cost competition of many outsourcing contracts (Grimshaw *et al.*, 2016). Unpicking the detail of aggregate statistics thus illustrates how employment is often more precarious than it initially appears.

The rise in NSFE and employment through subcontracting relationships have informed debate over job 'quality' as much as 'quantity'. Many NSFE jobs are characterised by little employment security, low pay, poor career opportunities and limited benefits. Several authors, such as Kalleberg (2011), Vosko (2010) and Standing (2011), have highlighted this rise in precarious employment. In particular, the latter has referenced the rise of a global 'precariat' of workers around the world as representing a potentially new and dangerous class. Precarious employment has also become a core concern among social partners and policy makers, both in Europe and in other developed economies. However, this rising interest has not resulted in a widely accepted definition of precarious work. In a study on 12 countries, McKay *et al.* (2012) found that there was no consensus about the meaning of precarious employment among key actors in the labour market. Many approaches try to 'unpack' precariousness into various aspects (e.g. McKay *et al.*, 2012; Paugam, 2005). For example, Grimshaw *et al.* (2016) discuss four protective gaps that capture the differences in employment conditions between different workers. This concerns gaps in regulation (e.g. minimum standards), representation (e.g. labour union membership), enforcement (e.g. lack of resources) and social protection (e.g. access to unemployment benefits and pensions).

A major issue relates to the voluntary or involuntary character of temporary employment. Some anecdotal evidence suggests that employees may prefer more flexible employment contracts because of their individual situations (CIPD, 2013; Robinson, 1999). For example, a recent initiative by McDonald's UK offered its workers on zero-hours contracts the option to move to fixed-hour contracts with a minimum number of guaranteed (or banded) hours, 'in line with the average hours per week they work' (Ruddick, 2017). The policy was trialled across 23 sites and 80 per cent of workers chose to remain on zero-hours contracts. Ostensibly, this could imply that the workers concerned are well served by their existing contracts. However, the example also illustrates how employees are often faced with restricted choices between different types of NSFE, or a band of new guaranteed hours which may be at unsuitable times of the day or evening. Arguably, when management re-structures hours and work choices with alternative options, this is not the same as a full-fledged preference.

Eurostat data confirm the involuntary character of part-time and temporary employment. For example, around 50 per cent of temporary workers in the European Union would prefer regular employment. Figure 2.4 presents data on temporary employment for a cross-section of European countries and shows that a substantial share of the workers in these countries accept this form of employment because of an inability to find permanent employment. The data for Germany suggests greater satisfaction among temporary workers but the lower percentages seem the result of a greater share of workers who combine temporary employment with education or training. Both the share of employees who did not want permanent employment and the ratio between those who could not find and those who did not want a permanent job do not suggest a greater preference for temporary employment. If we take this consideration into account, the similarities between countries are striking. The one exception is Spain and, in recent years, Croatia, where a large majority of temporary workers could not find permanent

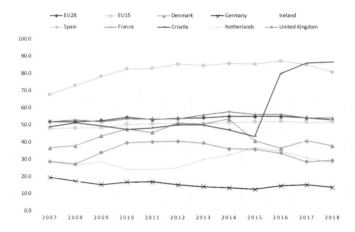

Figure 2.4 Involuntary character temporary employment ('could not find a permanent job'), 2007–2018

employment. Within the UK, the involuntary character of much agency work was particularly stressed by a TUC study in 2014.[3] It found that more than four out of every five agency workers between 20 and 24 years had been unable to find regular employment. While the percentages declined among older age groups, they remained over 50 per cent for all age groups between 20 and 59 years.

The data also confirms the secondary position of temporary workers in terms of earnings compared to those in permanent employment. Table 2.1 presents the most recent data available on the hourly and monthly earnings of temporary and permanent workers among the same group of European countries as included in the previous figures. All countries included indicate an 'earnings penalty' for male and, to a lesser extent, female workers in temporary employment. However, the penalty differs substantially between countries. The percentage share of hourly wages for temporary workers varies from 62 per cent for men in Ireland to 99 per cent for women in Denmark. Both Denmark and France stand out for the relatively small differences in earnings between temporary and permanent employees. Across countries, the penalty is lower for female workers but this is likely to be

Table 2.1 Earnings of temporary workers as a share of earnings of permanent workers (2014)

	Hourly earnings			Monthly earnings		
	Total (%)	Males (%)	Females (%)	Total (%)	Males (%)	Females (%)
EU-28	71	66	78	71	66	79
Denmark	91	83	99	84	77	92
Germany	72	69	79	74	71	81
Ireland	75	62	88	71	60	83
Spain	81	76	88	80	75	86
France	82	83	84	80	81	84
Croatia	65	63	69	65	63	68
Netherlands	68	64	74	68	63	74
UK	81	74	92	81	74	92

Source: Eurostat (https://ec.europa.eu/eurostat; earn_ses14_15; earn_ses14_22).

the result of lower wages for female compared to male workers in permanent employment.

The involuntary character and poor remuneration illustrate the secondary position of many temporary workers. Overall it has become clear that those in NSFE and employed through subcontracting contracts are likely to face little employment security, low pay, poor career opportunities and limited benefits (Grimshaw *et al.*, 2016). This is particularly problematic as many workers struggle to find better forms of employment; as several studies report, the norm is to fluctuate between low-paid temporary jobs and unemployment (Shildrick *et al.*, 2012; Wilson *et al.*, 2013). Echoing Doellgast *et al.*'s (2018) 'vicious circle' power elements as in Figure 1.3 in Chapter 1, insecure jobs constrain collective power solidarities which in turn leave workers as even further marginalised outsiders.

The impact of (digital) platform work

In this section, platform work (often referred to as the gig economy) will be used as an illustrative example of contemporary change and development, since platforms encapsulate a number of emerging labour market trends. Platforms leverage processes of globalisation and digitalisation to enable interaction between external producers and consumers and access an 'on-demand' workforce (de Stefano, 2016). Many commentators perceive platform work as a new form of work organisation and tend to focus on the divergence from more traditional employment. This is especially evident in the Taylor Review of Modern Working Practices, where recommendations for gig economy working dominates, despite the Review being commissioned to consider all work within the UK (Taylor, 2019). No doubt, novelty is evident with the emergence of global platform firms (such as Airbnb, Deliveroo, TaskRabbit, Uber and Upwork) offering diverse app-based services; however, much of the work itself shares many of the characteristics associated with NSFE. The activity often involves microtasks, which are menial, monotonous and highly fragmented (Howcroft and Bergvall-Kåreborn, 2019) and this represents the dominant – although not universal – feature of platform-based work. It has particular appeal to capital since it offers lower costs and numerical flexibility, which is partly achieved by classifying workers as 'independent contractors' (Berg, 2016) and also by the cost savings associated with operating in an unregulated environment. Compared with traditional employers, platforms are intentionally positioned as neutral intermediaries who merely facilitate a digital matching service between end-users, absolving them of any legal responsibility and social or moral obligations. This tripartite relationship raises difficult questions regarding who exactly constitutes the employer. Meanwhile, the platform designs the working environment, monitors behaviour (of workers and consumers), and digitally curates every transaction, at the same time as collecting big data.

Platform marketplaces have been permitted to grow in the shadow of the law, raising difficult legal questions about employment status and rights (Cherry, 2016) as Chapter 3 discusses. The evolution of platform-based working has outpaced regulation, which has led to numerous court cases in the United States and the United Kingdom. The majority of lawsuits are labour-related and contest issues of 'bogus' employment classification, whereby risk is shifted onto workers who are unprotected by minimum-wage legislation or any other workplace entitlements. Some platforms have deliberately adopted specific procedures to avoid triggering statutory definitions of employment, for example, preventing continuous work with one client (Lehdonvitra, 2016).

For the platform to achieve success it needs to assure consumers that a quality service will be provided, therefore effective control of a transient workforce comprising independent contractors is critical. This is achieved via various means. First, from the perspective of the platform, the self-employment classification not only provides employers with cost savings in the form of tax advantages, but it also mobilises commitment to quality work, since pay is withheld if the work does not meet the requisite standard. Second, tightly defined terms and conditions stipulate governance structures which clearly specify (the absence of) responsibility on behalf of the platform and ensure all transactions are in accordance with contractual terms (Bergvall-Kåreborn and Howcroft, 2014). Many platform workers are regularly forced to agree to new and highly complex terms of service whenever they log in to access the platform (Calo and Rosenblat, 2017). Finally, software algorithms, which are bestowed with legitimacy, impartiality and accuracy (Gillespie, 2014), are created to evaluate and manage interactions with minimal intervention. Algorithmic management (Lee *et al.*, 2015) allows platforms to oversee workers in an optimised manner over a large scale, often meticulously tracking participants in real-time. These algorithms are supplemented with user-generated evaluations that feed into the management of the workforce (Zwick, 2015) with some associated with race and gender discrimination (Slee, 2015). The intensification of monitoring and surveillance significantly undermines autonomy, ensuring control and capacities to influence ultimately lie with the platform. Specific features in the design of platforms provide a convenient method for establishing patterns of control, which minimises worker autonomy and results in glaring asymmetries of information and power (Calo and Rosenblat, 2017).

Platform workers have limited capacity to harness trade union representation as a form of influence (Brabham, 2012). They are either excluded from regulatory frameworks that enable collective representation or they experience difficulties in accessing and using them (Johnston and Land-Kazlauskas, 2017). Consequently, there are numerous barriers to collective organising. While platform workers use social media and forums to share information and discuss experiences, there is limited evidence of sustained action and critical mass (Salehi *et al.*, 2015). The lack of legal protection means that some are concerned with the risks that agitation may pose to their own reputation and the possibilities of being deactivated from the platform with associated loss of income. The substitutability of labour and the fact that new workers may join and leave the platform daily constrains capacity to leverage scarcity, so expressing discontent is perceived as futile and perilous. However, as the area matures, attempts to develop collective agency, representation and bargaining are beginning to surface (Johnston and Land-Kazlauskas, 2017). Platform workers are developing new strategies to cope with changes in employment patterns and the labour movement is increasingly engaging with attempts to promote fair, inclusive and secure labour markets for the growing ranks of gig workers. Chapter 4 addresses some of the new forms of worker voice that are emerging within these new spaces and the way they are using innovative forms of collective action.

The future of work debate and automation
The growth of NSFE and accompanying low levels of productivity have led futurologists to invest faith in new technology in the hope that this will signify economic transformation. In terms of the future of work debate, recent developments suggest that we are entering a 'fourth industrial revolution' (Schwab, 2016), which claims that 'we stand on the brink of a technological revolution that will fundamentally alter the way we live, work and relate to one another' (Schwab, 2016: 1). Technological innovation is seen to represent a digital tsunami that is evolving at an exponential pace, signifying a seismic shift from previous eras of sociotechnical change (Mason, 2016; Rifkin, 2014). Much of the recent interest among commentators, policy makers and academics centres on robotisation and automation, potentially impacting labour displacement as well as altering the content, the quantity and the quality of jobs.

The automation of work and employment is well-trodden ground for scholars of technology and work, with anxieties about the displacement of jobs dating back to the Luddites. While new concerns have resurfaced, the current instantiation of technological innovation is frequently lauded as being significantly different from the past. Commentators generate fear with their predictions that smart robots, aided by the provision of big data to support machine learning, signify the death knell for jobs. The highly influential book *The Second Machine Age* (McAfee and Brynjolfsson, 2014) has become an axiom for the forthcoming technological revolution as massive improvements in computing power have enabled advances in robotics and artificial intelligence which can now be used and applied in many different contexts, including the transformation of work. As the level of robotics use has almost doubled in the top capitalist economies in the last decade (Roberts, 2016), numerous concerns have been raised about the future of work.

However, alarmist outcomes are speculative and many are based on unsubstantiated predictions with little supporting evidence. Those leading the discussion on the implications of automation for the future of work adopt a number of different positions. One dominant group of pessimistic commentators fear a 'labour-light economy' (McAfee and Brynjolfsson, 2014) whereby workers are ousted by smart machines. For example, highly cited research on the US economy argues that that almost half (47 per cent) of total employment is in a high risk category that has the potential of being automated within the next 10–20 years (Frey and Osborne, 2017). Compared to previous debates regarding automation in the 1980s, current anxieties cluster around the displacement of high-skilled, highly educated labour with robots (Ford, 2015; McAfee and Brynjolfsson, 2017).

Other commentators, who acknowledge that significant number of jobs will be lost, suggest there is the potential to upskill work processes, replacing routinised and repetitive work with highly skilled roles and 'knowledge workers' (Willcocks and Lacity, 2016). Here there is an emphasis on the importance of education and training with the onus of responsibility placed firmly on the shoulders of individual workers who are expected to re-educate and adapt. While many view upskilling as the route to better jobs, research shows that increasing education and qualifications often leads to a mismatch, whereby workers are unable to find the most appropriate employment for their skills (Green and McIntosh, 2007). Finally, more radical and optimistic commentators welcome full automation in order to liberate people from the drudgery of work as investments in productivity-enhancing technologies increase wealth, which links to wider debates for advancing the provision of universal basic income (Srnicek and Williams, 2016).

Common throughout these various positions is an overall consensus that work will look very different in the future and the capacity for workers to influence their future remains contestable. These predictions, whether optimistic or pessimistic, are underpinned by technological determinism, whereby the technology is seen to be driving socio–economic change. The history of implementation and use shows that technological change does not emerge as *deus ex machina* but is rooted in prevailing socio-economic contexts and corporate decision-making. Although the declining costs of technology might suggest that employers have economic incentives to substitute labour with computer capital, in reality the pressure to deliver financial returns to shareholders can divert investments away from core business activities including longer-term technology capital investment (Cushen and Thompson, 2016). This is evident in declining investment levels in advanced economies, which have dropped by more than 13 per cent since 1990 (IMF, 2017b). If the pricing of labour is sufficiently low, then there is little incentive to invest in the automation of particular occupations. This is borne out by research in the United States, where only 10 per cent of the firms that could benefit from robots have opted to do so (Frey and Osborne, 2017).

A further problem with technological determinism is the assumption that technology is neutral while technological systems are infused with politics, particularly arrangements of power and authority. Employment relations are replete with examples whereby automation is introduced with the intention of diminishing the power of resistant or striking workforces, such as dockworkers and car assembly workers. Winner (1980) illustrates this point well using the example of the reaper manufacturing plant in 1880s Chicago. Ostensibly introduced to modernise the plant and bring efficiency gains, new machines operated by unskilled labour were introduced to destroy the Union of Iron Molders and obviate the need for skilled labour, since these workers had played a pivotal role in organising the union. After three years, it was evident that the new technology resulted in inferior casting at higher cost but the implementation had achieved its objective: destroying the union. It seems fair to assume that decisions to automate will be made in the context of employment relations, with capital opting to supplant the more fractious elements of labour.

Corporate decisions to invest in technology are also political decisions and so much of the investment in automation has led to labour reductions in strongly unionised workplaces such as car manufacturing plants. However, the process of labour displacement has been far from straightforward. Examples from companies such as Audi, BMW and Mercedes-Benz show that some robots are now being replaced with employees since robots cannot handle the complexity of key customisation options. Tesla, famous for electric cars and seen as being at the forefront of the technological revolution, has resorted to replacing robots with humans as 'excessive automation' has led to an overly complex web of processes and a failure to hit production targets. The fact that car manufacturing, which is the one of the most advanced adopters of robotics, is having to revert back to employing humans suggests that automation is far from straightforward.

Finally, amidst the debate on the future of work, there is a glaring issue that is conveniently swept aside: rather than new technologies creating job losses on a massive scale, unemployment remains low in many Western economies. While high employment levels appear positive, aggregate level statistics mask the more subtle labour market changes outlined in this chapter, which includes increasingly precarious work with more commodified forms of labour with low pay, insufficient and variable hours, short-term contracts and limited social protection rights (Rubery *et al.*, 2018). For this reason, placing degradation at the forefront of debate is critical to the shaping of the future of work, as opposed to speculative concerns that robots will wipe out the workforce.

Conclusion

This chapter began by looking at the organisation and disorganisation of capitalism in order to provide historical context for contemporary debates about work and employment, particularly decreasing levels of worker influence. This was then examined in relation to globalisation, financialisation and technological change in order to provide understanding of how wider structural shifts are shaping and influencing employment relations. Emerging from these changes is flexibilisation as a defining characteristic of developments in employment forms. While the impact of this is wide-ranging and affects many workers, those positioned in NSFE and those employed through subcontracting have encountered particularly precarious working experiences. We thus see the manifestation of fragmentation as a negative trend, with diminished capacity for people to influence the terms under which they work. Even those in more 'stable' employment are increasingly vulnerable and subject to rising levels of work intensification. For those in a weakened labour market position, platform or gig economy work may seem to offer some respite when faced with poor pay levels and in-work poverty, but this type of work epitomises many of the characteristics associated with NSFE. The threat of job loss through automation can affect bargaining power, as the narrative of 'robots are coming for our jobs' is presented as an inevitability. If jobs are fragmented, and workers have weak contracts and limited employment rights, then it will be far easier to automate. However, as discussed, technology reflects society but does not determine it: employer choices, labour organising and legal debates have the potential to reconfigure outcomes in a more positive direction. Some of these debates, including how the role of the state affects power and influence at work, will be considered next in Chapter 3.

Notes

1 A specific type within the EU is posted work which refers to 'jobs filled by migrant workers who are employed by a company or an employment agency that is registered in the migrants' home country and is part of a chain of cross-border subcontracting' (Grimshaw *et al.*, 2016: 215).
2 Employees with temporary contracts are those who declare themselves as having a fixed-term employment contract or a job which will terminate if certain objective criteria are met, such as completion of an assignment or return of the employee who was temporarily replaced.
3 TUC, 'More than two-thirds of agency workers aged under 30 are looking for permanent jobs, says TUC', www.tuc.org.uk/economic-issues/labour-market-and-economic-reports/labour-market/economic-analysis/more-two-thirds [accessed 9 August 2016].

3

The state, law and equality

Introduction

In this chapter, we focus on three interrelated factors that affect workers' ability to influence their employment relationship and which are therefore critical determinants of the balance of power between capital and labour. The first addresses the general nature and changing role of the state as a social and institutional actor and the extent to which it has undermined the role of worker voice through the decollectivisation of employment relations. The second focuses on a key dimension of the state by considering the role of the law per se in terms of policy positions on legal intervention in employment relations, the individualisation of labour and employment rights, and questions of access to justice and the attribution of legal rights in an ever more fragmented world of work, with particular reference to the 'gig economy'. This chapter looks mainly at the case of the United Kingdom as an example of some of the mostly draconian changes to worker rights in terms of de-regulation, although the patterns are of relevance globally. Finally, the third part explores dynamics of change and complexity in relation to the subject of equality (or rather institutional and structured inequality and institutional responses to it) and related issues in employment, looking in particular at labour migration and gender inequality in relation to worker influence, outlining some of the complex and contradictory developments of recent changes in the role of the state.

The chapter applies a WES perspective to widen our view of how the body of worker rights has shifted and contributed to the challenges and changes in the forms of worker voice. It recognises the fundamental imbalance of power within the system of employment relations that leaves workers in a more vulnerable position. It also looks at the contradictory effects of legislative and policy reforms by showing how they have recently weakened the positions of workers socially and not just economically and legally. The 'double whammy' of reducing worker rights socially and politically whilst simultaneously reducing the enforcement of the traditional and hard-won rights they rely on – as well as new ones as we explain in terms of employment equality – means that we need to understand the political context of regulation. Such an approach is informed by contemporary debates within WES on power and politics at work.

The role of the state as a work and employment relations actor

The state is a highly complex and unique employment relationship actor. In addition to being a legislator, the state fulfils several roles that help shape the balance of power between various actors. It functions as an enforcer of workers' rights, as an economic manager, as a social actor directly and indirectly creating jobs and social services, as an employer in its own right and as a coercive force relating to work and employment relationships policy (Hyman, 2008; Martínez Lucio and MacKenzie, 2018). These broad roles contribute to the shaping of relations between the state, the employers and the workers. Moreover, broader economic policy can contribute to shifts in the business environment that contextualise labour relations. For example, the steady decline of manufacturing-based employers – who were previously highly unionised – can weaken this section of capital and undermine their presence in state policy-making processes. Along with a decline in trade union involvement in corporate state bodies (although never developed in the United Kingdom to the same extent as in Sweden or Germany, for example), the changing context and political orientation of the state means that worker-oriented traditions may be undermined. However, that does not mean that governments and agencies of the state will not occasionally intervene at key points or in high-profile issues, as seen with the Tata Steel case in the United Kingdom where the government was forced to intervene in some capacity in response to threats of closure (Ruddick, 2016).

This section focuses on the various ways in which the state (mostly using the United Kingdom as illustration of power and politics) has undermined the role of worker voice. We offer a general overview of the direct attempts to decollectivise worker voice and then broaden the analysis by outlining how the declining presence of the state in social terms has reinforced such changes. However, tensions emerge and the state has to constantly (re-)intervene to correct the negative impacts of political and economic developments, including those instigated by itself.

The changing role of the state

The roles and functions of the state are significantly important when considering power and politics in employment. The changes we have witnessed since the mid-1980s have begun to shape an environment where worker voice is weaker and more fragmented than it was during the post-Second World War era – although we should be cautious and not assume there was some simple 'golden age' of worker and trade union engagement unequivocally supported by the state (Hyman, 2008).

For many workers, a shift in the state's orientation away from a collective rights-based framework has altered the framework of employee voice and engagement (Williams and Scott, 2016). The emergence of legislation that undermines the role of collective voice is a significant factor in debilitating the way trade unions can use collective action and engage with collective bargaining (Howell, 2005). Attempts have been made by various governments – in the United Kingdom, in particular, since 1979 – to weaken the reach of collective forms of negotiation and trade union roles (McIlroy, 1991). This neoliberal and market-based ideology has also shaped recent policies in various EU member states, such as Spain, that since 2008 propagated the removal of certain forms of collective rights on matters related to collective bargaining and worker dismissals although not to the extent of the United Kingdom. Such de-regulation is premised on the assumption that the state should allow management greater prerogative in the pursuit of so-called 'efficiencies' and 'flexibility' (Martínez Lucio *et al.*, 2017; Martínez Lucio and MacKenzie, 2018). Coupled with new business models and increasing insecure work contracts, the broader role of the state is highly impactful on peoples' working lives. Michael D. Higgins, the president of Ireland (2019), has been vocal in articulating the unequal consequences on a global scale of such work arrangements:

> We are now witnessing increases in precarious employment, contract working, and an ongoing casualisation of labour … I see this trend as part of an inexorable 'race to the bottom', and I believe that further regulation, together with enforcement, is urgently required in order to protect those most vulnerable in society from being exploited as a result of the most adverse effects of these new forms, falsely described as work, but often forms a dependency relationship without rights.

The weakening of labour market institutions (e.g. inspectorates and related enforcement bodies) have been observable in a range of contexts and countries, with that 'race to the bottom' facilitated given the failure of the state to protect those in fragmented and more hostile workplaces. Worker voice in such contexts has been undermined as workers are unable to draw on the labour enforcement mechanisms of the state in what are becoming 'hard to reach' workplaces (Mustchin and Martínez Lucio, 2020). This is not to suggest that trade unions and social organisations have not responded politically to such developments, quite the contrary. However, the extent and depth of worker influence has been constrained in different ways.

The emergence of de-regulation policies has impacted on specific categories of more vulnerable workers and diminished their influence; for example, female workers have been disproportionately undermined within the workplace given the declining levels of state support in social and familial terms (Karamessini and Rubery, 2013). Such developments undermine the access many groups of women may have to stable employment and workplaces where there is, typically, a greater possibility to develop their organisational role and voice. The shift in the state towards more market-oriented policies, together with a greater emphasis on a reduced social and welfare domain, means that workers are finding their ability to develop the time and resources for the development of their civic role within organisations increasingly restricted, as the next section will examine.

The changing social character of the state

There is a tendency to view labour law as being the main factor framing workers' rights on collective participation and their ability to pursue individual grievances. However, developments in broader welfare and labour market policy can also shape employee input into work-related decisions and, in the specific national context of the United Kingdom, erode it. For example, attempts by the state to force workers with disabilities or the long-term unemployed into work by withholding or altering their welfare benefits can have contradictory and unforeseen outcomes, let alone erode the social wellbeing and health of those at whom the policies are directed (Karanikolos *et al.*, 2013). If restrictive welfare policies are pursued in such a way that it leads to greater poverty, it may generate greater levels of social isolation as a worker's ability to participate in broader social activities may be reduced. Furthermore, the increasing presence of working environments that abuse the vulnerability of 'welfare to work' employees can produce a state of affairs where such workers are deterred from taking an interest in a greater collective engagement and voice within the workplace, or even preclude them from doing so. One could, supposedly, also argue that the experience of such working conditions could lead to militant political responses and radicalisation processes among such workers; however, the growing vulnerability of the workforce may undermine their ability to engage and participate within traditional forms of worker and social representation. Increasingly, such types of workplace may not have effective or collective systems of worker representation to start with. Clark and Collings (2018) have shown how certain employers have exploited vulnerable migrant workers in workplaces such as hand car washes. This stimulates a highly intensive and unsocial working environment that can undermine the ability of workers within the workplace to contribute and engage with their employing organisation on more positive terms (although we cannot assume that such a participatory objective is central to these types of employer in the first place).

The welfare policies of the state – when coupled with the labour relations policies of anti-trade unionism – may, therefore, reinforce a workplace culture based on direct forms of management control and poor working conditions, thus restricting the scope for worker engagement both socially and politically within the workplace and beyond. Other chapters in this book have focused on the problems with new forms of workplaces and the sheer pressures and levels of work intensification that exists within them, but these can create a culture where communication and engagement – and voice more generally – are undermined. They are undermined by state mechanisms that create a culture of coercion where individuals may be forced into certain types of employment that limit self-development and personal development, both as a worker and as a citizen. These 'bleak house' working environments have become more common in the face of new types of employment in the gig economy. The continuing use of ethically problematic forms of worker blacklisting and surveillance by the state and employers – which can shift and severely restrict employee influence within the workplace (Smith and Chamberlain, 2015) – is indirectly enhanced by restrictive welfare policies. The general reduction of welfare and social provision puts a greater onus on individuals in terms of their abilities to support themselves and their family, given the impact of more time-consuming travel to work as they navigate a fragmented labour market and individually coping with a more hostile psychological context at work. This leads to a general reduction in the time and resources workers have for social and political activity both at work and beyond. Sennett (1998), for example, argued that the growing levels of work intensification and insecurity can lead to a destabilisation and fragmentation of local and social communities. There is a real cost to society as a whole brought about by a system of employment where democratic roles and capabilities are undermined: and this in turn feeds back into the workplace and undermines democratic engagement by workers.

The rise of the dysfunctional state

Importantly, such shifting state dynamics may not be uniform or common across national contexts, or even within them. Ultimately, these contextual features of the state have varied. Much may depend on the relative balance of power between workers and employers, as well as contextual forces such as the extent of financialised capitalism and neoliberal economic doctrines within any particular country. Hence, we cannot generalise in terms of how the state is undermining the voice and participation of workers both directly and indirectly. The next chapter on trade union engagement and roles clearly outlines the continuing differences in the way workers are represented in the sphere of the firm throughout Europe. There remain quite varied levels of works council and company-based participation, as well as trade union membership (see Chapter 4).

It is being argued that there is a creeping – or encompassing – neoliberalism within even the more coordinated market economies. Baccaro and Howell (2017) contend that the post-war Fordist model of regulation with collective representation and wages has been fundamentally altered in recent years, even in cases such as Germany where there are ever greater challenges to collective bargaining coverage. In Sweden, the de facto decentralisation of collective bargaining is increasingly common in terms of the new trade-offs being made between wage increases and more flexible forms of working. To some extent, Baccaro and Howell (2017) seem to be less optimistic and more concerned with the way ideological and economic practices of neoliberalism have been shaped and systematically extended. There is evidence to suggest that the discourses of neoliberalism – in terms of the questioning of labour rights, which are increasingly seen as social and economic rigidities – have been extended in many parts of the European Union even with its formal interest in social rights. This is especially the case in those countries of the European Union that have been most exposed to the 2008 financial crisis as economic support has been conditional on the adoption of various policies that deregulate aspects of the labour market (Koukiadaki et al., 2016; Martínez Lucio et al., 2017).

The state and the aftermath of de-regulation

We have to be somewhat cautious in sustaining the view that, across various dimensions, the role of the state has been systematic or deliberate in undermining voice. The outcomes of such strategies are clearly tilting the balance of power and control towards employers, but there are contradictions within these shifts. The developments outlined present a series of contradictions and challenges for the employer classes and management, let alone for organised labour and workers. The fragmentation of voice in terms of a more decentralised and limited system of collective bargaining can undermine the complex institutional relations within joint regulation that manage workplace conflict. Marginalising the reach of more established trade unions, especially those with a tendency towards social dialogue, ignores a wide range of negative outcomes for employers and the economy. It can lead to a greater politicisation of employment relations and a greater tendency to see industrial conflict as a way of representing the demands of workers. As Wright Mills (1948) pointed out, trade unions can be important to the channelling and managing of 'discontent' on behalf of capitalists. The extensive wave of restructuring and de-regulation in southern Europe since 2008, for example, has not engendered high levels of workplace trust, employee engagement and systematic or sustainable increases in productivity (Koukiadaki *et al.*, 2016); if anything, broadly speaking, there has emerged a greater level of individual conflict and worker grievances through the juridical dimensions of the state (Kirk, 2018; Martínez Lucio *et al.*, 2017). The idea that worker voice can be easily dismantled or undermined without there being unexpected or unintended outcomes of a problematic nature for the state is naive, to say the least.

Hence, the idea that the state has simply withdrawn from a direct role and developed a more concerted effort at limiting worker voice, through various forms of social and industrial interventions that undermine collectivism, ignores the way the state has had to respond to the negative outcomes for both workers and even employers of its policies of industrial relations de-regulation. The need to 'prop up' in some form or another the role of workers as an active agent in the firm has led to various initiatives in public policy aimed at developing micro-corporatist (Alonso, 1999) and supply-side approaches to industrial relations.

First, to some extent we have seen the sphere of training and development being used as a space for enlarging trade union and worker representative roles. The changing and complex nature of skill sets and the need for more flexibility have been a focus of public employment policy within the European Union and even in the case of the United Kingdom, albeit to a lesser extent (Stuart, 2007). Joint trade union–employer involvement in training is one way of allowing mutual gains for both management and workers to evolve and for new forms of social dialogue to emerge (Kochan and Osterman, 1994). There are many critics of this supply-side and market-oriented form of trade union behaviour, as it can create dependency on the firm and the state where public funding for training is channelled through trade unions (McIlroy, 2011). Problems can emerge when there are weaker guarantees provided to the trade union movement in terms of its role and systems of representation within such processes and more generally (Martínez Lucio and Stuart, 2004). However, there have been various attempts to provide a certain organisational space in such areas of economic activity as training and development as a way of linking workers back into firm-based discussions.

Second, it has not been unknown for the state, in cases where there have been more sympathetic governments, to provide support to trade unions in terms of their attempts at innovation in relation to the more dispersed and fragmented labour market. The support for information centres for precarious and unprotected workers in Spain (Martínez Lucio and Connolly, 2012), or a greater number of broader innovations in worker representation and engagement in vulnerable communities (Stuart *et al.*, 2013) have been a growing feature of various industrial policies. They do not, in themselves, represent a substantial reconfiguration of worker voice or a return to a more collective tradition of industrial relations, but they do allow for experimentation to occur in relation to the form of worker voice. Through 'consultative/educational' roles, the state has, to some extent, also attempted to steer employers and trade unions into adopting specific mutual gain strategies; for example, the development of social dialogue, trade union–management partnerships, new forms of team-working and so on (Martínez Lucio and Stuart, 2011). In those contexts where there has been greater de-regulation in industrial relations, the state has not necessarily returned to some 'golden age' moment of collective regulation; however, we cannot discount the internal contradictions within public policy as it grapples with the tensions and outcomes of its own policies of greater marketisation and change (see Martínez Lucio and MacKenzie, 2018).

Employment law as a contested terrain

We now move on to consider one traditional manifestation of state power and influence, that is law and formal regulation where we see similarly contradictory developments. Labour/employment law and regulation in the UK, however, may best be seen as a product of the interplay between various national (and international/regional), institutional and social actors in specific but constantly changing historical, social, political, legal, cultural and economic contexts (Kahn-Freund, 1977; Lewis, 1976). The relevant actors and institutions currently include the European Union, the state, employers, employers' associations, employees, trade unions and the judiciary. The latter plays a critical role in developing key areas of the UK common (that is, judge-made) law around, for example, the contract of employment and also interpreting and applying parliamentary legislation and regulation. Legal sources can thus exist in a variety of different forms, including common law, acts of Parliament, regulations and directives, often supplemented by codes of practice and/or guidance.

Historically, the development of employment regulation has been and remains 'contested terrain' in public policy-making and political debate, demonstrating ongoing shifts in power and influence. Therefore in this section we address evolving perspectives and policy positions on employment law, supra-national influences, questions of access to justice, power resources and the critical issue of employment status that determine employment rights.

Perspectives on legal regulation

To understand these continuing debates, it is thus necessary to consider perspectives on the 'essential' nature and purposes of legal regulation. A well-respected perspective posits that the individual worker has little choice other than to accept the conditions that the employer offers:

> [T]he relationship between an employer and an isolated employee or worker is typically a selection between a bearer of power and one who is not a bearer of power. In its inception it is an act of submission, in its operation it is a condition of subordination, however much the submission and the subordination may be concealed by the indispensable figment of the legal mind that is the contract of employment. (Kahn-Freund, 1977: 6)

Over the last few years there have been echoes of this insight in an increasing number of UK judicial decisions – up to and including the Supreme Court decisions in *Autoclenz* v. *Belcher* (2011) and *R (on the application of Unison)* v. *Lord Chancellor* (2017). In the latter case, Lord Reed (delivering the sole judgment of the Court) explicitly stated that 'relationships between employers and employees are generally characterised by an imbalance of economic power. Recognising the vulnerability of employees to exploitation, discrimination and other undesirable practices, and the social problems which can result'. This has led, he continued, to parliamentary intervention over time to 'confer statutory rights on employees, rather than leaving their rights to be determined by freedom of contract'.

An alternative perspective argues that the dominant objective of employment law is to 'improve the competitiveness of businesses so that they may survive and prosper in an increasingly global economic system' (Collins, 2001: 18). However, there are widely divergent views in the literature on the best way to achieve this objective. The view that has largely dominated employment law and policy in the UK for almost four decades is that 'competitiveness is best achieved through deregulation of the job market, leaving business free to discover the most efficient solutions to production problems' (Collins, 2001: 18). However, it is equally arguable that 'social dialogue' coupled with state intervention could correct an imbalance of power towards employers and, by doing so, steer business 'towards the most efficient relations of production' (Collins, 2001: 18).

There has been widespread agreement and acceptance over recent times that the UK job market remains 'one of the most lightly regulated' among leading economies (DBIS, 2013; DTI, 1998). Indeed, this view is reinforced by the OECD database (2014) which shows the UK to be second only to the United States as the most *lightly* regulated of *all* OECD countries. Despite this, much policy-making has been based on an alleged 'reality' that perceives employment laws to be 'one-sided', favouring employees, and that 'the cost and complexity of employment laws impact on their ability to take on staff and grow' (Peck *et al.*, 2012). However, there is good evidence to suggest that these views have often been misplaced and based largely on employers' anxiety and fear, rather than 'any actual experience and perpetuated by the pervasiveness of the "anti-regulation" discourse occurring in the wider society' (Jordan *et al.*, 2013: 44). Indeed, in a report for the Department of Business, Innovation and Skills (DBIS), Jordan *et al.* (2013) surveyed employers on employment regulation and found a 'perception–reality gap'. That is to say, employer references to 'burdensome' regulation stemmed more from employer anxiety and perceptions around the complexity of the law, rather than the existence of legal obligations or excessive constraints per se. This raises significant questions as to whether regulation could be simplified and whether sufficient support structures exist to enhance employer understanding about their legal obligations and eliminate feelings of uncertainty.

Power and legal regulation

There has nevertheless been a trend towards greater 'juridification' of and legislative intervention in work and employment relationships over time in terms of scope, content and substance (Clark, 1985). In the UK, for example, the scope and content of individual employment protection legislation has expanded over the last 50 years or so to many areas of the employment relationship, including unlawful deductions from pay, the National Minimum Wage (NMW), working time and paid holidays, fixed-term employment and agency work, discrimination, redundancy payments and unfair dismissal (Deakin and Morris, 2016). Indeed, UK employment tribunals (ETs) now categorise their workload under some 54 distinct jurisdictional codes. A number of these and other developments have been influenced by the UK's membership of the EU. In relation to the scope of legal rights, however, there remains continuing debate over the categories of workers to which legislation is applied (see further below).

The depth of legal content can be observed in the context of what Kahn-Freund (1977) described as 'auxiliary' legislation, governing the regulation of collective employment relationships more broadly. While for a period up until 1979 in the UK such legislation was broadly supportive and/or permissive of the UK's 'voluntary' system of collective bargaining and employment regulation (Dickens and Neal, 2006; Flanders, 1974), it has subsequently and more recently been aimed at restricting the capacity and ability of trade unions to take industrial action, most recently exemplified by the Trade Union Act 2016 (Ford and Novitz, 2016). There is also a growing disconnect between collective rights, which are in decline, and an emphasis on fragmented individual rights (Howell, 2005).

A possible approach to narrowing this disconnect is suggested by the Institute of Emplyoment Rights' (IER) *Manifesto for Labour Law* (Ewing *et al.*, 2016). This posits a largely two-pronged approach: (1) the redefining of employment relationships, granting all employment rights from day one of employment and making those rights more accessible and easily enforceable; and (2) re-establishing national collective bargaining through Sectoral Employment Commissions (SECs) 'with responsibility to promote collective bargaining and to regulate minimum terms and conditions of employment within specific industrial sectors of the economy' via Sectoral Collective Agreements. SECs would be comprised of equal numbers of employer and employee representatives, with a lesser number of representatives from a new Ministry of Labour where this may be necessary to break deadlocks (Ewing *et al.*, 2016: 20).

The concern about weakened collective rights is addressed as a matter of policy in the IER Manifesto, adopted by the British Labour Party, as the basis for a number of its policies on industrial strategy and rights at work and, as such, featured significantly in the party's 2017 and 2019 election manifestos. Among other things, these undertook to 'repeal the Trade Union Act 2016 and roll out sectoral collective bargaining – because the most effective way to maintain good rights at work is collectively through a union'. This is in turn redolent of Kahn-Freund's (1977) contention that, in relation to the inherent power imbalance already referred to, 'for labour, power means collective power'.

Supra-national factors, politics and power

Power and influence is also potentially leveraged by various international/supra-national actors. At the global level, reference must be made to international employment law sources: conventions, standards and principles developed since 1919 by the ILO, within a 'tripartite' structure involving member states, employers and worker representatives (Blanpain, 2014). Individual states voluntarily choose to adopt 'law' and it may be viewed as lacking any meaningful depth in terms of formal process or institutional structure for enforcement (Blanpain, 2014; Hepple, 2005; Weiss, 2013), even where a state is found to be in consistent breach of ratified conventions (in the UK context see, for example, Ewing, 1989). To some extent, it may be argued that global standards have been 'privatised' (Royle, 2010) and are mainly disseminated with varying shallow forms of voluntary, informal and 'soft law' mechanisms, including multinational codes of conduct (Alhambra *et al.*, 2011) and international framework (collective) agreements (Dehnen and Pries, 2014; Mustchin and Martínez Lucio, 2017).

In contrast, the body ('acquis communitaire') of supra-national EU social and employment legislation is part of the fabric of the law of member states (see Barnard, 2012). The critical issue at present in the UK is the potential or likely impact of leaving the EU (for a detailed legal analysis of the issues, see Ford, 2016). The European Union (Withdrawal) Act 2018 (EUWA) provides simultaneously for the repeal of the 1972 European Communities Act and the incorporation of the full acquis communautaire of *existing* EU law into UK domestic law, including the decisions of the Court of Justice of the European Union (CJEU), as at the date of leaving. The continuing supremacy of EU law is thus ended following departure but the body of EU legislation and case law immediately prior to that date is 'retained'. After this date, section 6(2) of the EUWA provides:

> A court or tribunal need not have regard to anything done on or after exit day by the CJEU, another EU entity or the EU but may do so if it considers it appropriate to do so.

The final part of this provision was subject to considerable criticism during the passage of the act through Parliament, particularly regarding clarity and precision, not least by the outgoing President of the Supreme Court, Lord Neuberger (Rawlinson, 2017).

Perhaps even more significant is the future of existing EU legislation on employment and labour rights. Much of this legislation (especially in areas such as working time and paid holidays) has been something of a focal point in many of the deregulatory debates already discussed. It is therefore of some concern that Schedules 7 and 8 of the EUWA provide for the possible repeal and/or amendment of this and other 'retained' EU law (and EU law incorporated into UK primary legislation such as the Equality Act 2010 [the EqA 2010]) after leaving by means of secondary legislation (i.e.

statutory instrument), with a short-circuited process involving limited parliamentary scrutiny. In this regard, we can only rely on the
following broad statement of intent: 'The Government's approach
to workers' rights is clear – it has merely indicated that it will protect workers' rights, and to seek out opportunities to enhance protections when that is the right choice for UK workers. The EUWA
itself will ensure that EU-derived employment rights will continue
to be available in domestic law after the UK has left the EU.' At
present, however, this has only manifested itself in a rather limited
commitment to allow parliament to vote on *whether* the UK should
accept any new or improved EU rights into UK law in the future
(DBEIS, 2019). Indeed, the uncertainty around the future direction
of employment rights will undoubtedly continue, as there seems to
be little appetite for any significant or ongoing regulatory alignment
with the EU as the UK exits the European social model.

Access to justice and enforceability of rights

Fundamental issues around power and influence recur when considering the effectiveness of employment law and access to justice
which affect employee capacity to leverage change over working
conditions. As trade union membership and collective bargaining
coverage (especially in the private sector) has declined in the UK
(see Chapter 4 for density data), the historical trend towards the
juridification of employment relationships has led to a greater prolif-
eration and 'individualisation' of rights. Problematically, this means
that the burden of enforcement has to a large extent been placed
on individual employees and workers (Ewing *et al.*, 2016) within
a 'victims complaint, self-service approach' (Dickens, 2012). It is
clear, however, that for many workers these so-called 'rights' exist
in the realm of the theoretical and illusory rather than the practical.

ETs were originally established on the principle that they should
be 'an easily accessible, speedy, informal and inexpensive procedure for the settlement of … disputes' (Donovan Commission,
1968). This has been used historically to justify limited state support via legal aid and advice for those wishing to bring ET claims.
However, the increasing complexity of both the law itself and the
procedure for bringing claims has fundamentally undermined the
original goal of ETs. It has become clear that, as stated recently

by the Joint Committee on Human Rights (Joint Committee on Human Rights, 2018), 'there are large areas of the country which are "legal aid deserts", as practitioners withdraw from providing legal aid services since they can no longer afford to do this work following reductions in legal aid funding by successive governments over the past three decades'. And even in the sole remaining area of Discrimination where legal aid remains theoretically available, no clients were referred and/or advised face-to-face under the legal aid scheme in 2016/17.

There are also significant problems about the advice and support available for the increasing numbers of workers and employees who are not union members, resulting from the massive decline in voluntary and/or third sector advice agencies such as law centres and the Citizens Advice Bureau (Legal Action Group, 2016). Unfortunately, this problem will not be solved by the seminal decision of the Supreme Court in the *Unison* case in July 2017 (above) that led to the abolition (at least for the present) of the 'controversial' ET fees regime (see Walden, 2013). The Court ruled that the regime was unlawful under both the UK common law right of access to justice and EU law. While there has undoubtedly been a significant increase in the number of ET claims following this decision (for example, an increase of just under 109 per cent in single claims in the period January–March 2017 to January–March 2018 but still some 30 per cent or so below the pre-July 2013 figures before fees were introduced), this does not address the fundamental problem of the disparity of resources or information available to the claimants.

One method of addressing such deficiencies would be the development of alternative dispute resolution mechanisms and/or further state support for individual or group enforcement. Such provision already exists, for example, in relation to HM Revenue & Customs' (HMRC) role in enforcing the NMW. In addition, HMRC has some role in resolving disputes about statutory sick pay through its 'statutory payment dispute team'. There is now also a Labour Market Enforcement agency,[1] whose role is to set overall labour market strategy and priorities for three of the four state enforcement authorities: the HMRC, the Gangmasters and Labour Abuse Authority and the Employment Agency Standards Inspectorate (EAS). Its first annual report (2018) emphasises the

need for 'clear and accessible information on employment rights' to
be provided to workers through a number of channels. The government (DBEIS, 2018a) has also broadly accepted the proposal contained in the Taylor Review of Modern Working Practices (Taylor,
2017) that the state should enforce 'a basic set of core rights' (in
essence the NMW, statutory sick pay and paid holiday entitlements)
for 'the most vulnerable workers'. In particular, the government
proposes to introduce a new state enforcement system for holiday
pay and will identify the most appropriate body for doing so. It
also proposes among other things to extend the right to receive a
statement of employment particulars to all employees *and* 'workers',
with an expanded list of key information to be provided on day one
of employment (i.e. not just within the first eight weeks as is the
case at present). This latter change was due to be implemented in
April 2020.

It is, however, argued in some quarters that this does not go far
enough: the IER Manifesto (Ewing *et al.*, 2016) suggests that 'new
methods of enforcing (individual) labour rights should be introduced'. These would be based on the power of a newly established
Labour Inspectorate, together with other state bodies and trade
unions, to initiate legal proceedings on behalf of workers. Further,
workers given notice of dismissal would in the first instance be able
to refer the matter immediately to a senior labour inspector, who
after an expedited hearing should have the power to annul the dismissal and order the reinstatement of the worker (if the dismissal
has already taken place).

The impact of changes in contract status

Elsewhere this book reviews literature relating to market factors, the
role of the state, issues of non-standard and precarious forms of
employment, together with the potential 'protective gaps' to which
this may lead. Our immediate concern here is to review how the
UK employment law system recognises, understands and adapts to
these changes.

Conceptually, the 'fundamental institution' in UK employment
law remains the concept of the 'employee' under an individual
'contract of employment' (Wedderburn, 1986). But this is essentially a creature of the common law, with essential and required

characteristics identified and developed over time by the judiciary, including a sufficient framework of control by the employer, obligations on the putative 'employee' to wholly or mainly perform work personally and an ongoing 'irreducible minimum' of mutuality of obligation on the employer to offer work and the employee to accept it when it is offered. Unfortunately, such characteristics assume a degree of uniformity and consistency that is often found only in traditional standard forms of direct and permanent employment. It is also worth noting that in common law there is a 'systematic dichotomy' between the contract of employment (or service) and the similarly unitary 'contract for services' (that is, self-employed independent contractors – see Freedland, 2003). The contract of employment therefore remains the primary vehicle for distributing and attributing rights, with *only* employees enjoying access to *all* available statutory employment protections, including for example unfair dismissal and redundancy payments.

In parallel, recent decades have seen UK legislation provide additional definitions of employment status to which a more limited range of statutory rights apply. Most particularly, those defined as 'workers' attract the protection of, principally, NMW legislation, the Working Time Regulations 1998 (WTR) – including minimum paid annual leave – and the provisions on unlawful deductions from wages. The scope of this contract status extends beyond the core contract of employment to cover any contract under which an individual 'undertakes to do or perform personally any work or services for another party' (e.g. reg 2(1)(b) of the WTR – commonly known as 'limb (b) workers') and is not carrying out a business vis-à-vis a customer or client.

How far the 'worker' definition extends the coverage or scope of protection is not always obvious. Literatures informing such issues include legal case law as well as academic analyses. Case law, for example, confirms the intention to create an 'intermediate' class of workers who are substantively and economically in a similar position of dependence to that of employees (*Byrne Brothers* v. *Baird*, 2002). One key pointer is whether the purported worker actively markets their services as an independent person to the world in general, or whether they are recruited by the employer to work as an integral part of the employer's operations (*Cotswold Developments*

v. *Williams*, 2006). In addition, courts and tribunals have tended to take a holistic approach which recognises that the degrees of control and/or mutuality of obligation are substantially less for workers than those required for employees (*Adkins* v. *Lex Autolease*, 2017). These distinctions create continuing questions as to where to draw the line between these factors.

To add further confusion, there is yet another statutory definition of 'employee' that applies in discrimination cases. The EqA 2010 prohibits discrimination against those in or seeking 'employment' which means 'employment under a contract of employment, a contract of apprenticeship or any other contract personally to do work or labour' (s.83(2) EqA 2010). This would appear to cover an even wider category of labour providers than the 'worker' definition just outlined. It has focused on whether the 'dominant purpose' of the contract is the execution of personal work and, if so, it seems likely that the relationship will be a case in which the person concerned performs services for and under the direction of the other party to the contract in return for remuneration. This may not be so however because, although the dominant purpose of the contract may be personal work, it may not be personal work under the direction of the other party to the contract. There is thus a clear distinction between those who are, in substance, employed and those who are independent providers of services who are not in a relationship of subordination with the person who receives the services. The essential questions are whether, on the one hand, the person concerned performs services for and under the direction of another person in return for which he or she receives remuneration or, on the other hand, whether he or she is an independent provider of services who is not in a relationship of subordination with the person who receives the services (see *Jivraj* v. *Hashwani*, 2011). For example, in *Jivraj* itself, an arbitrator appointed by the parties under a commercial contract was found not to be a person employed under a contract personally to do work for either of them.

Attempts at evasion and the judicial response
Against this backdrop of uncertain (or insecure) worker status definitions, there have been well-documented attempts by some less scrupulous employers to deny statutory rights by seeking to

reframe the written terms of the contract to preclude employee and/or worker status. Denying statutory rights has taken various forms, including bogus self-employment as discussed in Chapter 2, with written terms purporting to negate the personal service and/or mutuality of obligation requirements (*Autoclenz* v. *Belcher*, 2011) or, in the extreme, representing each pair of employees as being in an independent 'partnership' of which the employer was the 'client' (*Protectacoat* v. *Szilagyi*, 2009). Contract status is not about individual employee preferences for any type of work but rather the scope of mutual and reciprocal employment obligations between two parties. To this end, literature suggests that even zero-hours contracts that do not guarantee any minimum number of hours may be seen in a similar light. It is arguable that in the strictest sense they cannot amount to a continuing contract of employment and, in one case, it was suggested that 'it was doubtful whether [a zero-hours contract] amounted to any contract at all' (*SW Global Resourcing* v. *Docherty*, 2012). On the other hand, where such a zero-hours contract *is* found to amount to an ongoing contract of employment and the employer effectively suspends the employee without pay and without contractual authority, the employee is entitled to their average pay based upon the previous period of work actually completed (*Obi* v. *Verma and Rice Shack Ltd*, 2017).

Notwithstanding some worker rights, the most high-profile examples of alleged evasion of obligations have arisen in the gig economy, in particular in relation to Uber drivers and cycle couriers, among others (see below). In the face of very limited legislative intervention to address such issues (limited so far to the prohibition of exclusivity clauses in zero-hours contracts), the judiciary has stepped into the breach as an unexpected source of solace for workers, with attendant implications for the balance of power between the parties. While courts and tribunals have in theory always been required to take account of the 'reality' of employment relationships and not just the written terms of contracts (*Young and Woods Ltd* v. *West*, 1980), the former element has increasingly been given prominence in recent years. For example, in *Szilagyi*, the Court of Appeal found that the purported partnership arrangement was a 'sham' and in no way reflected the reality that the individuals were in fact (and in law) employees. This approach was endorsed by the Supreme Court

in *Autoclenz*, based on a recognition of the 'imbalance in bargaining power between employers and employees' and the fact the latter
often have little or no choice other than to accept the terms offered
by the employing organisation (see further Bogg, 2012).

The same principles have been applied to the judicial interpre-
tation of the statutory definition of the 'limb (b) worker'. In *Aslam
and Others* v. *Uber BV and Others* (2016), the ET roundly rejected
the argument presented by Uber that it was not providing a trans-
portation service and was merely a platform for connecting self-
employed drivers to clients. It found that drivers were workers when
the Uber app was switched on in the territory in which they were
authorised to work and when they were willing to accept assign-
ments. Referring to *Autoclenz*, the employment judge condemned
Uber's resort to 'fictions', 'twisted language' and 'brand new termi-
nology' in an attempt to mask reality. This decision was upheld by
both the Employment Appeal Tribunal (EAT) (2017) and the Court
of Appeal (2018), with the caveat that in general the assessment of
a driver's status and time in between the acceptance of individual
trips would always be a matter of fact and degree but the ET was not
wrong to decide as it did in this case.

Similarly, in *Dewhurst* v. *Citysprint* (2017), the ET found that
allegedly self-employed cycle couriers were 'workers' and found
that there was 'a clear inequality of bargaining power and the true
situation is very different from that portrayed in the tender, starting
with the name of the document itself as there was no tender "process" at all'. The ET case of *Lange and Others* v. *Addison Lee* (2017) –
a case involving allegedly 'self-employed' drivers – similarly agreed
that 'the contractual provisions, when analysed objectively, do not
properly reflect the true agreement between the parties'. This decision was upheld by the EAT in November 2018. In *Addison Lee
Ltd* v. *Gascoigne*, the EAT (2018) found that allegedly self-employed
cycle couriers were under a workers' contract 'during the log-on
periods with the requisite mutual obligations'.

A key element in a number of these cases has been the existence of so-called 'substitution clauses' purporting to exclude core
'employee' or 'limb (b) worker' status. In the latter regard, the
leading authority is the judgment of the Supreme Court in *Pimlico
Plumbers* v. *Smith* (2018). Here the Court held that the 'dominant

feature of Mr Smith's contracts with Pimlico was an obligation of personal performance. To the extent that his facility to appoint a substitute was the product of a contractual right, the limitation of it was significant'. The judgment in *Pimlico Plumbers* casts considerable doubt on the only decision running contrary to the general trend in favour of gig economy 'workers', that of the Conciliation and Arbitration Committee (the CAC) in *Independent Workers' Union of Great Britain (IWGB)* v. *RoofFoods t/a Deliveroo* (2017). In this case, the CAC found that the 'central and insuperable difficulty for the union is that we find the substitution right to be genuine … and we have heard evidence, that we accepted, of it being operated in practice'.

Proposals for reform?

It has been argued that some workers may actively choose various forms of non-standard and flexible work, such as zero-hours or if-and-when contracts (CIPD, 2015), as we discussed in Chapter 2. However, policy debates suggest that neither employers nor workers benefit or achieve certainty when the courts determine employment status ex post facto, and largely on a case-by-case basis. Such considerations led to one of the key proposals contained in the Taylor Review of Modern Working Practices (Taylor, 2017). In essence, it proposed renaming 'limb (b) workers' as 'dependent contractors' and giving greater emphasis in this regard to the element of 'control' as opposed to the obligation to provide labour or services personally. Extensive analysis or research arising post-Taylor is, at the time of writing, limited. Nonetheless, commentary has argued that this seems like 'reinventing the wheel', given the approach being taken by the judiciary to the 'worker' definition (e.g. Kirton, 2017). Further, Bales *et al.* (2018) observe: 'that amending the term "worker" … would create unnecessary complication and further confusion … the term "dependent contractor" denotes a degree of subordination which, at present, is not a necessary requirement for categorisation as a worker'.

The government response to the Taylor Review of Modern Working Practices proposes to legislate to 'improve the clarity of the employment status tests, reflecting the reality of modern working relationships' and the need for some alignment with their application for tax purposes (DBEIS, 2018a). However, the IER Manifesto (Ewing *et al.*, 2016) goes significantly further. It would essentially reduce the choice to that between all 'workers' (including employees) and those operating businesses on their own account in order to attribute full and universal (what are now) core 'employee' rights to the former from day one of employment. Accordingly, it would establish a new definition of the 'labour provider' (Countouris, 2018) covering (at the very least) both 'workers' and 'employees'. Countouris also expresses concern that resort to categorising many of those in the gig economy as limb (b) workers – with the attendant limitation on employment rights – has become something of a 'default' position.

In other areas, Taylor proposed rights for agency workers to *request* a 'direct' contract of employment, where they have been placed with the same hirer for 12 months, and for those on zero-hours contracts to *request* a contract that better reflects the actual hours worked where they have been in post for the same period. The government has actually committed to introduce a right for 'all workers to request a more predictable and stable contract' that should apply after 26 weeks of employment (DBEIS, 2018a). However, this would amount to a 'soft' right akin to the right to request flexible working. There is also a proposal to repeal the so-called 'Swedish derogation' which allows for agency workers directly employed by the agency itself to be excluded from equal pay with the client organisation's permanent staff. It has to be said, however, that the overall impact of the Taylor Review of Modern Working Practices' recommendations and the consequent government proposals do not appear to favour the capacity of workers to alter or influence their employment status or rights in any substantial direction.

Regulating for equality (or inequality)

Finally, in this chapter, we discuss the issue of equalities in the workplace as a key part and example of the way the state intervenes in key areas of the employment relation and which affects power and influence. Two reoccurring themes within existing research include how social, economic and cultural exclusion is structurally reinforced by regulatory regimes, and how government policies could be altered to enable particular social groups to harness deeper influence, thereby creating a more inclusive society.

Labour migration and questions of worker influence

Many countries have experienced increases in migration in recent years, largely stemming from intensified global economic activity, financialisation and flexible labour structures (Dundon *et al.*, 2007; Marino *et al.*, 2017). In the UK, a key force influencing the increasing presence of migrant workers more recently has been the 2004 A8 expansion of the European Union, which opened the UK labour market to individuals from the A8 nations of Central and Eastern Europe (Dawson *et al.*, 2017; McCollum and Findlay, 2015). At the same time, government immigration policies across European states have become more negative and xenophobic, in part since the 2008 financial crisis and subsequent recession (Tilly, 2011). In the UK, the Immigration Acts of 2014 and 2016, serve as two examples of anti-immigration policies which inhibit migrant access to essential elements such as housing, education and employment. Within UK policy, the term 'migrant' is elastic and complex as no single measure exists. First, an individual can be defined as a 'migrant' by length of stay, foreign citizenship or foreign birth (Tapia and Alberti, 2018). Furthermore, a migrant's status varies, shaping their right to work and employer recruitment strategies (Cangiano and Walsh, 2014). For instance, non-EU migrants may secure a working visa enabling them to access the labour market for a specific period while asylum seekers generally have no right to employment. Migration status also differs among EU nationals, for example between the self-employed, students and job seekers, which again moulds their experience of the labour market (Tapia and Alberti, 2018).

For the reasons outlined above, an 'intra-categorical' approach has been advanced to the study of migration (Tapia and Alberti, 2018), where differences between sub-groups of migrants and how they experience social processes of discrimination and segregation. Relatedly, research on migration tends to engage with low-skilled migrants and their unfair exclusion, while neglecting high-skilled migrants. This is unsurprising given that the low-paid economy has become increasingly reliant on migrant workers as a form of disposable, cheap labour. However, the labour market experiences of high-skilled male and female migrant workers also require attention (Liversage, 2009; Van den Broek *et al.*, 2015). Moreover, the UK's catalysing decision to leave the EU is highly likely to have repercussions on the employment situation of high-skilled migrants and future labour migration flows. Thus, an 'intra-categorical' approach considering the multi-level nature of the intersectional processes of labour inequalities and how they foster distinct and overlapping experiences within and between migrant groups is important (Tapia and Alberti, 2018). There are thus ramifications in terms of worker influence and associational power, as there is a degree of fragmentation within migrant communities and with the so-called indigenous workforce – a broad category in its own right. Questions of exclusion, segregation and exploitation within work and in employment varies between these communities, raising challenges as to how such interests link through any forms of representation and systems of solidarity or social exclusion (Connolly *et al.*, 2019).

A macro-level neoliberal policy agenda has been key to explaining non-EU nationals' vulnerability to intense employer control and exploitation at workplace-level. For example, one key barrier heightening the plight of non-EU nationals in the Republic of Ireland was the work permit system, which at the time inhibited migrants from changing employers (Dundon *et al.*, 2007). This shows how employers abuse their positional power to use structural rigidities of the work permit system as a covert threat over workers (Anderson and Ruhs, 2010). Consequently, migrants are unlikely to challenge management for fear of reprisal. Managerial power to exercise discretion over the continuity of non-EU nationals' employment contracts and, through this, their rights to remain in the country, are severely constrained and union capacity to represent them made more difficult.

Relatedly, although many state immigration controls (e.g. work permits) are often peddled by the government as shielding migrants from exploitation, in reality the particular immigration regime in a country can undercut labour protections. It has been argued that immigration controls serve as a mould helping to generate particular forms of workers, including 'more desirable' workers who have little choice but to tolerate inferior working conditions (Anderson, 2010). Moreover, the way in which immigration controls subject individuals to high levels of institutional uncertainty render employers with intense power controls they cannot exercise over other citizens (Dundon *et al.*, 2007).

During the Lindsey Refinery strike that took place in the UK in 2009, institutional mechanisms fomented labour inequalities and gave rise to deep social divisions, pitting migrants and citizens against each other (Ince *et al.*, 2015). Contractors took action because of employer attempts to use migrant workers as a way of cutting costs. The terms and conditions of UK construction workers are covered by the National Agreement for the Engineering Construction Industry (NAECI). Overall, the minimum conditions for workers under this agreement are higher than the minimum legal requirements as offered to the posted (migrant) workers. The major fractures between the sets of workers were patent during the strike, for example, some workers utilised the 'British Jobs for British workers' slogan, illustrating how employer actions result in divisions and weaker worker solidarities (recall Figure 1.3 from Chapter 1).

A fundamental problem during the Lindsey Refinery strike was how the EU Posted Workers' Directive was transposed into the UK's regulatory system. The Directive intended to force employers to treat migrants equally to citizens of their host country, with regards to their minimum standards of employment. However, the Directive has been incorporated into UK legislation in such a way that the term 'minimum standards' for contractors equates to minimum legal requirements, for example the national minimum wage, not the minimum standards set by the NAECI (Ince *et al.*, 2015). This provided employers at Lindsey Refinery with the potential capacity to substitute British contractors with an immigrant workforce on inferior terms and conditions. However, these problems have not been specific to the UK. A dispute between the Latvian construction company Laval un Partneri, and Swedish trade unions, over the use of cheaper Latvian labour, shows how significant regulatory loopholes and a lack of clearly specified legal working conditions eroded worker protections intended by the Directive (Woolfson and Sommers, 2006).

While migrant workers may 'strategise' to travel to the UK, Datta *et al.* (2007) show how the persistent social and economic constraints they encounter upon arrival, such as labour market segmentation, low-pay, de-skilling and a lack of additional benefits (e.g. sick pay, pension, compassionate leave, overtime pay), means their behaviours are better classed as fragmented and fragile 'tactics'. Such tactics can be cross-cut by other social relations such as class, gender, ethnicity, and may include reorganising their household economies, establishing alternative networks and discovering other means of income. The latter could involve claiming state benefits but only 17 per cent of migrants within Datta *et al.*'s (2007) sample did this, despite 91 per cent paying tax and national assurance. This may be partly because of the complex legislative system outlining an individual's eligibility to apply for benefits.

In terms of trade unions and more formal voice mechanisms there has been a steady move from less engaged approaches to migrant communities towards a more inclusive and representative dynamic (Fine and Tichenor, 2012). However, this expansion of the role of trade unions can vary in terms of the way they are included within trade union structures (e.g. the role of black worker sections in the UK), the way community information centres address and support migrant demands (Spain), or the way social partnership strategies extend established rights through trade union negotiations at the state level (the Netherlands) (Connolly *et al.*, 2019). In addition, we are seeing new forms of worker representation and campaigns that are more independent of the mainstream bodies of trade unions – this new, more agency focused approach is important to understand the greater flexibility and dexterity in terms of union voice and representation (Alberti and Però, 2018). These developments illustrate how it is important to provide a more dynamic and realistic view of the way migration impacts on questions of worker influence to allow for matters of agency to be included and the possibility of the renewal of forms of worker representation to be better comprehended. Hence, we need to consider the way the state interacts with migrants and workers' organisations in different and sometimes contradictory ways.

Gender equality and the challenges of change

A significant area of policy and regulation where the contradictions of state policy are evident is the question of gender equality. Scholars (e.g. Rubery and Fagan, 1995) have sought to reverse the gender bias in comparative industrial relations and encourage researchers to extend their focus beyond male manual worker regimes, arguing that the gendered character of employment relations needs deeper recognition. A promising shift has occurred in recent years where gender equality has gained significant attention. This shift is understandable considering that the number of women employees and union members continues to increase and that gender equality has become a key objective for unions (Hebson and Rubery, 2018).

The relationship between union activity and gender equality objectives warrants analysis. For instance, the increase in equal pay claims registered before employment tribunals in Britain during the 2000s advanced an equality agenda and provided tangible gains to disadvantaged society groups, but only in the presence of a well-functioning collective bargaining system with formal pay structures (Deakin *et al.*, 2015).

A study of 134 female union leaders in America and Britain found that in an internal and external environment hostile to women, a collective gender identity motivated the long-term participation of female leaders to some extent, but that a collective union identity was more dominant (Kirton and Healy, 2013). The collective gender identity was contested because not all women members supported or identified with gender-based union strategies (an example could be pushing for new legislation to promote gender equality). Feminist values and principles were advocated to a greater extent among British than American leaders, but most of the union leaders felt that prioritising 'bread and butter' issues such as redundancies, pay, other benefits and health and safety problems was key, particularly against a backdrop of union decline.

Work–life balance and gender

Gender equality is linked in the literature to issues around work–life balance, social reproduction and the unpaid domestic work many females engage in, irrespective of their employment status (Hebson and Rubery, 2018). Regulating long hour working is therefore argued to be particularly important for women, but must vary across occupations (e.g. between informal economy workers, factory workers and professionals who determine their own working arrangements); and be combined with more affordable childcare and elderly care services (Fagan *et al.*, 2012).

Organisations today often offer part-time work contracts and claim that these arrangements demonstrate their commitment to enhancing female work–life balance. Yet, the way part-time work and female demand for such working arrangements differs across European states is largely shaped by the historical exclusion of females from or integration of females into labour markets. For instance, females in Germany were traditionally discouraged from working because of the nature of the tax system. On the other hand, women in Nordic regimes were more integrated into the labour market and received high benefits and leave entitlements to encourage labour market participation (Hebson and Rubery, 2018). In Germany and the Netherlands, part-time work has been utilised to encourage females who traditionally had a housewife role to participate in paid employment. In the Nordic country of Finland however, the historical tendency for women to work full-time has continued (Pfau-Effinger, 1998), but part-time working has increased in recent years. Opportunities to work part-time are a 'double edged sword' (Fagan *et al.*, 2012). On the one hand, they can help females juggle work and caring responsibilities. However, they may also direct females towards a thin segment of female-dominated occupations and reinforce both labour market gender segregation and the role of females as 'primary carer' at home. In this context the role of the state is key in regulating and overseeing these developments – see Chapter 2 for a similar discussion on how flexibility and non-standard work varies throughout Europe.

One gender equality issue that has recently captured attention is the need for gender equality in parental leave policy so that fathers are entitled to the same level of parental involvement as mothers. The opportunity for mothers and fathers to take shared parental leave came into force in the UK in 2015, as a means of capacitating fathers to better integrate work and family life. The new rights enable parents to share up to 50 weeks of leave, with 37 weeks being paid at £140.98 (2017–2018) a week, or 90 per cent of a worker's average weekly earnings (whichever amount is smaller). The shared parental leave scheme also permits greater flexibility to parents in terms of when they take their leave. For instance, each parent is entitled to three 'blocks' of leave interspersed with working periods (DBEIS, 2018b).

However, government estimates imply that only 2 per cent of fathers have utilised the shared parental leave initiative since its introduction. Two key potential reasons why include: (1) the loss of earnings after taking parental leave, given fathers are more likely to constitute the primary breadwinners in households; and (2) shared parental leave decreases the amount of leave mothers are eligible to take (Barlow, 2018). Furthermore, the shared parental policy includes eligibility criteria (Davis, 2017).

The 'Fathers and the Workplace' enquiry (Parliament UK, 2018) recommended in 2018 that fathers are given an independent statutory right to 12 weeks of parental leave, including four weeks at 90 per cent of their salary (but a cap for high earners) and another eight weeks at a statutory pay rate. However, despite being a significant step forward, there are barriers restricting active implementation (e.g. organisational factors, a lack of awareness and cultural constraints). Arguably, the reality is that the statutory pay level is so low it is often unrealistic for many fathers to take parental leave. Additionally, some fathers feel uncomfortable taking parental leave due to the fact that it is traditionally taken by females (Barlow, 2018). Similarly, despite policy advances aimed at supporting men's increased involvement in childcare, in reality, fatherhood is overlooked in workplace settings, and, in the literature, men are predominantly characterised as breadwinning workers, rather than active fathers (Burnett *et al.*, 2013).

In terms of worker influence and voice, there remain gaps in terms of the role of women in areas such collective bargaining and representation. Even when the voice of women in trade unions has been developed through various forms of networking, there are still questions of hierarchy and exclusion (Healy and Kirton, 2000). Yet there are some forms of renewal and change. For example, the role of female trade union officers is important for balancing traditional and male-oriented objectives (Kirton and Healy, 1999). Gender equality strategies are often able to influence the long-term strategic renewal of trade unions and worker voice although there are clearly ongoing challenges (Kirton, 2015). There are a range of employment issues related to leave, care or promotion which have seen a significant input from trade unions and related bodies – even non-government organisations as we show later. However, there remain challenges in extending the language and practice of equality, especially when faced with public policy prescriptions for austerity and global geo-political uncertainties (Durbin *et al.*, 2017).

Furthermore, while the recent 'MeToo' movement (#MeToo online campaign) renders a promising example of global solidarity among females against sexual harassment and violence, it has also foregrounded the profound failure of organisational structures and legislation to shield women from abuse, and uncovered the pervading fear which often prevents them from speaking up. In 2018, workers in unorganised corporations including McDonalds and Google staged #MeToo protest walkouts. In McDonald's for example, hundreds of employees staged lunchtime walkouts in ten American cities over the company's failure to address a sexual harassment epidemic. Workers were inspired by the '#MeToo' campaign, but also endeavoured to underscore that the abuse, harassment and coercion suffered by low-paid employees deserves the same level of attention and coverage as the high-profile celebrities that have been the campaign's harbingers. McDonald's workers explained how employees who depend on such precarious jobs fear that reporting harassment will risk their employment, legal status and lead to retaliation (Lydersen, 2018; Rushe, 2018). Hence when discussing these issues of equality and personal treatment the role of the state in terms of legislation and policy is important: but of equal importance is how these laws and policies are used in different ways or not referenced within the day-to-day reality of working lives. The other important point we need to remember is that whilst the state is attempting to withdraw in, or weaken, certain areas of employment rights it keeps being drawn into dealing with the consequences of change and the call for greater fairness (see Rubery (2011) for a discussion of these tensions).

Conclusion

WES perspectives view the role of the state as an essential actor in any discussion on worker rights, power and politics: yet a WES perspective sees it also as an ambivalent one. The state provides the formal framework of rights and responsibilities within employment and therefore serves as a key political force, with the capacity to protect workers from structurally unbalanced manager–employee power relations, but also to reinforce the unequal employment relationship exchange. Yet, this political, regulatory context is subject to significant change and open to a set of contradictory developments. We have seen how in terms of legal rights the UK represents one of the main examples of de-regulation and liberalisation. The chapter has focused on how there has been a so-called hollowing-out or undermining of collective rights with workers being exposed to an employment relation where collective voice is increasingly removed or marginalised, thwarting employee power whist feeding employer control. In terms of various sets of individual rights, we have also seen the way the notion of being self-employed has been mobilised by the state to reconfigure the very meaning of what a worker and employee is. The onus of responsibility falls on the shoulders of the worker themselves with employer responsibility for an array of social aspects of work being changed and often removed. This reshaping of the concept of the employee – and issues of employment protection – has run in parallel with serious challenges to the way the state supports the articulation of rights and their development. Access to legal services and to state enforcement mechanisms have been fundamentally reduced, such that even those rights that continue to exist within the employment relation as potential vehicles of employee power are difficult to operationalise individually and collectively. In addition, how state policy and law is used within the employment relations often depends on the capacity and resources of the workforce and its representatives.

This shift in the political landscape and the role of labour law has been facilitated by a decline in the regulatory reach of the state's agencies. The nature of the state is complex: it consists of many actors and institutions that aim to underpin the development and realisation of worker rights. Yet these agencies have been reduced in their scope and influence. Even the reduction of the social role of the state is having repercussions for the ability of workers to have a say or an input into work-related issues. The sheer degradation of what one could call the realm of labour reproduction is undermining worker power to intervene in social and public spheres within work, although the state has not disappeared from the arenas of work and employment due to constant calls for fairness and the need to address much of the 'fall-out' from its own policies (Rubery, 2011). These raise concerns as to who actually speaks for workers in such a fragmented context, discussed next in Chapter 4.

Note

1 The first (and previous) director was Professor David Metcalf, formerly of the London School of Economics.

4
Who speaks for whom at work?

Introduction

Worker voice is perhaps the most politicised and power-centric of all WES issues. An eminent scholar many years ago, Alan Flanders (1970), articulated the point that 'for management to gain control, they must first learn how to share it'. Thus, the very idea of having a say about work-related issues is a contested space, subject to various power struggles and forms of regulation and control, as well as hidden agendas and control strategies (see Wilkinson *et al.*, 2020). In this chapter, we discuss four approaches affecting 'who speaks for whom' at work. We categorise these as: 'institutional influences' (e.g. works council regulations); 'union power' (e.g. collective bargaining), 'non-union voice' (e.g. internal company communications), and 'external agency beyond the workplace' (e.g. civil society groups, associations, co-operatives).

The argument is that while worker voice has become fragmented and disjointed as many employers undermine unions and collective bargaining, union campaigns have been resilient and other advocacy groups signal new innovative spaces to help leverage more positive worker contributions.

Institutional 'influences'

Works councils
One of most recognised institutional influences for workers to have a voice is through mandated 'works councils'. Rogers and Streeck (1995) differentiate between three types of works councils. First,

there are 'paternalistic councils', established to provide welfare support to workers; but they can also be a tactic used by corporations to avoid unions (which we discuss later). Second are 'consultative councils', established as a voluntary arrangement to improve cooperation between managers and employees. The third type, 'legally mandated works councils', operate in countries such as Austria, Germany, Spain and Belgium. In such countries, works council election procedures are stipulated in national law, including provision for a defined term of office for employee representatives, the number of hours they can spend on works council affairs, office facilities, and training for worker representatives so they can do the role effectively. Works councils can encompass employee and employer representatives in some countries like Belgium, while in other countries (e.g. Austria and Germany), works councils include employee representatives only (Degrauwe *et al.*, 2018).

The capacity of works councils to support worker influence depends on the type of participation rights: *informational*, *consultative* and *co-determination*. First, information rights indicate that employers must share 'information' with worker representatives, for example, financial information pertaining to acquisitions, mergers, takeovers and yearly balance sheets. Information only rights can result in weak power-sharing, as managers retain a significant degree of authority to implement strategies and plans without even asking for employee opinions (Rogers and Streeck, 1995). Consultation rights indicate that works council representatives must be informed by managers about company plans and, importantly, be permitted an opportunity to 'share a considered response or counterproposal'. Although still providing managers with power to implement decisions, consultation rights permit somewhat deeper influence for workers than mere informational arrangements alone. The issues works council representatives must be consulted over vary by legal rules in different European member states, but they often include things like work changes, new technology, health and safety and redundancy threats (Degrauwe *et al.*, 2018).

Legislation in some countries (e.g. Austria, Germany, the Netherlands) also furnish another form of power, that of co-determination rights. Co-determination signifies that works councils can veto managerial plans or strategies relating to particular issues and a binding decision is then made by a court, or conciliation board, to resolve the issue. For example, works councils in Germany enjoy deeper influence than any other member state. Their co-determination rights cover a wide scope of aspects including social issues (e.g. work hours allocation, health and safety, monitoring employees through technology), personnel issues (e.g. recruitment, holidays, employee transfer) and economic issues (mergers, acquisitions, relocation, significant financial changes) (Degrauwe *et al.*, 2018). However, that is not to say that voice arrangements are flawless in Germany. In fact, there is a wage-productivity gap where productivity is increasing, but wages are not increasing at the same pace, indicating a power struggle over these issues within the operation and functioning of works councils.

It has been argued that providing collective voice to workers through mandatory works councils can generate a rent-producing effect by decreasing worker quit rates; and a rent-seeking outcome by rendering opportunities for workers to regulate labour supply and boost wages (Nienhüser, 2020). Furthermore, works councils may create a high-trust working environment and enable managers to harness greater employee co-operation (Rogers and Streeck, 1995). In other words, worker voice through the institution of a works council can be economically efficient for corporations, and may enhance trust and mutual respect in a workplace.

Voluntary joint consultative committees

Many countries (UK, Ireland, Australia, New Zealand and the United States – among others) have no statutory works council system. Similar mechanisms, often known as joint consultative committees (JCCs), staff or company councils, or office committees, exist in some contexts. However, usually, these are voluntary, and therefore are very different to the works councils in the above section, which have legal backing. Some JCCs in the UK have emerged as a response to the European Union's interest in worker participation. The 2004 ICE regulations, transposed from the European Directive (2002/14/EC) on *Employee Information and Consultation*, stipulates the establishment of workplace mechanisms for managers to: (1) provide information to their employees and/or their representatives about the economic situation of the organisation;

(2) provide information and engage in consultation on issues relating to organisational developments; and (3) consult with an intention to reach an agreement on threats to employment, or changes to work contracts (Dundon *et al.*, 2014b; Hall and Purcell, 2012). Yet, the regulations only apply in particular contexts and the fact the UK will be withdrawing from the EU means these rights for workers may diminish in the future.

As things stand now, in the UK, the regulations are only enforceable in organisations with more than 50 employees. In addition, the consultation mechanisms must be triggered through a written request from 2 per cent of an organisation's workforce (following the recommendation of the Taylor Review) or a minimum of 15 employees.[1] Employers can choose whether to count a part-time worker as half an employee or not and casual/agency workers are excluded. In terms of power and influence, these trigger conditions can place undue stress on workers, who do not wish to be seen as challenging or questioning management by asking for the right to information and consultation. Fearing employer reprisals is highly probable in non-union organisations where union support for workers is absent (Cullinane *et al.*, 2017), or in organisations with weak unions. A further limitation is that managers can claim pre-existing communication arrangements in a company as a way to stave off legislation or weaken a worker's request for information and consultation. Crucially, the so-called 'pre-existing' arrangement may be individual communication mechanisms, rather than collective voice structures, as intended by the original Directive (Hall *et al.*, 2011). Additionally, the Directive does not provide statutory rights for employee representatives to organise pre-meetings, attend training and use office facilities. These aspects depend on management goodwill, which may be in short supply in organisations facing intense competition and/or globalisation pressures. Evidence shows that less than 20 per cent of UK companies have a JCC at higher organisational levels, and as few as 7 per cent of firms have a workplace level JCC (Van Wanrooy *et al.*, 2013). These figures have remained constant for a decade or more. Furthermore, the range of issues that JCCs can influence has declined over time (see Table 4.1). In other words, the scope of issues that employees can have a say on has declined over time.

Table 4.1 Scope of joint consultative committees (percentages)

Issue	2004	2011
Production	48	46
Employment	76	74
Financial	63	66
Future plans	75	77
Pay	62	55
Leave and flexible working arrangements	64	52
Welfare services and facilities	57	69
Government regulations	56	35
Work organisation	71	69
Health and safety	79	76
Equal opportunities and diversity	56	42
Training	68	54
Other	5	13

Source: Adam *et al.* (2014: 34).

Decline in the scope of joint consultation for workers can be partly attributed to governments actively favouring minimal legal rights, as discussed in Chapter 3. Governments in various countries have become captivated by a dominant neoclassical or orthodox economics perspective; policy makers seem engrossed with employers being able to choose voluntary options for worker voice. Building on Lukes' (2005) faces of power discussed in Chapter 1, it may be argued that managers and the state have shaped macro-level worker voice processes to enable employers to secure 'power over' workplace decisions, and dominate the regulatory space in more latent or less observable forms (Dundon *et al.*, 2014b). Employers actively engaged in political lobbying and tactical agenda-setting to directly shape the regulations that favour a more neoliberal free market agenda supporting employer power by undermining union bargaining (McDonough and Dundon, 2010).

Union power

The second group of approaches when considering who speaks for whom at work is trade union power. As noted above, many institutional arrangements are designed to underpin unions (although as we suggest later they can be used or developed to bypass unions). Whilst it is well known that union membership (as a union power proxy) has diminished over the last few decades and that across many countries, trade unions have faced severe attacks from an array of hostile and anti-union laws and corporate policies that weaken their capacity to mobilise members (Gall and Dundon, 2013), their role remains significant. As illustrated in Doellgast *et al.*'s (2018) framework from Chapter 1, trade unions remain key independent actors with potential capacity to generate worker solidarity and redress power imbalances, especially for migrant and other typically marginalised workers (Connolly *et al.*, 2019). For example in January 2018, Ryanair, a celebrated anti-union organisation, was required to recognise the trade unions for its pilots due to collective campaigning against the company. In addition, in May/June 2018, McDonald's and TGI Friday's workers participated in widespread strike action, for the first time ever, in a sector typically renowned for low unionisation, along with a global Google workers' walkout over demands for more equitable treatment.

Importantly, union decline does not in any way indicate that workers prefer non-union voice channels. In a national representative survey of American workers, Kochan *et al.* (2019) found that around 50 per cent of non-union employees (49 per cent of non-managerial workers and 48 per cent overall) desire union representation, signalling an ongoing and significant 'voice gap' (the difference between how much voice workers expect to have over their work, and how much they actually have). Further, the 48 per cent who would vote for union representation if given the opportunity had increased from around one-third in a previously similar 1995 survey (Kochan *et al.*, 2019). Of interest is the type of unionisation that can leverage influence, and this is considered next.

Forms of union influence

Summarised from different international sources, Table 4.2 outlines numerous forms of union influence, multiple influence levels and potential worker (member) gains.

Another form of potential union power is influence through networking with civil society organisations (CSOs). Although a fairly new phenomenon, potential for collaborative relations

Table 4.2 Union forms, levels and possible outcomes

Forms of union influence	Levels	Possible outcomes
Grievance advocacy	Individual	• Resolution and potential adaptation of company policy
Industrial action	Workplace/national	• Collective agreements
Moderate action/action short of a strike (overtime bans)	Workplace/national	• Collective agreements
Collective bargaining	Workplace/industry	• Collective contracts/agreements
Leveraging of commercial pressure and organisational reputation in supply chains	Industry	• Industry-specific legislation (that is, the Australian *Road Safety Remuneration Act 2012*) • Joint employer–union enforcement mechanisms
Use of law other than employment law	Industry	• Environmental regulation/criminality law
Political lobbying about industry policy	Industry	• Public investment in the industry, industry-specific job market initiatives
Political affiliations	National	• Social pacts
Test cases	National	• Changes to employment law
Living Wage campaigns	National	• Changes to the social wage
Global union federations	Supra-national	• International framework agreements
Participation in multilateral forums such as the ILO and EU committees	Supra-national	• EU directives • ILO conventions

Source: Adapted from Kaine (2020: 176) and Heery (2009).

between unions and CSOs has become an area of academic interest. Crucially, interactions between unions and CSOs can be complex, involving co-operation, conflict and indifference (Meardi *et al.*, 2019). Nevertheless, partnerships between unions and CSOs can be a promising form of union influence in particular contexts, as will be elaborated in the section on 'external actors beyond the workplace'.

Regulation and the role of the state, as discussed in Chapter 3 and Doellgast *et al.*'s (2018) framework, are major forces affecting the power and politics of union influence. For example, France has one of the highest levels of collective bargaining coverage compared to other OECD countries (98 per cent), largely because regulation facilitates industry-level collective bargaining (OECD, 2017). Compared to the United Kingdom or United States, with less than one-quarter of the labour force in union membership, industry-level bargaining is much more extensive in protecting workers in other countries like Germany and Portugal, even though actual union membership may be lower: 18 per cent union density in Germany in 2015; and 16 per cent in Portugal (OECD, 2017).

What do union representatives do?

What unions and local activists do at the workplace shapes power and influence. Table 4.3 highlights three significant points about

Table 4.3 Issues union reps spend their time on (percentages)

Issue	Union reps
Discipline or grievance	78
Health and safety	69
Rates of pay	61
Pension entitlements	55
Staffing levels	54
Hours of work	54
Holiday entitlements	47
Equal opportunities	44
Training	36
Performance appraisal	39
Recruitment or selection	31

Source: Van Wanrooy *et al.* (2011: 17).

potential power and influence from union representative roles. First, union representatives have some degree of influence over a wide scope of important issues (e.g. pay, health and safety, grievances etc.).

Second, unions help improve peoples' non-monetary terms and conditions. This links to a renewed focus in work and employment research on 'moral economies' and how workers have varied needs and motivations (Bolton and Laaser, 2013). Third, representatives spend most of their time on 'discipline' and 'grievance' issues for their members, indicating that union representatives help redress injustice from tighter performance-driven control in recent years (Kirk, 2018; Taylor, 2017). Contemporary debates centre on how far workplace representatives and unions collaborate with management, or redistribute resources away from employers to members. A newer development in this area is possible collaborative 'union–management partnerships', briefly discussed next.

Union–management partnerships

Partnership between employers, employees and their unions is a contentious issue in WES (Martínez Lucio and Stuart, 2005). Some authors, like Kelly (1998) and Danford et al. (2013), contend that for strong union power, they should avoid establishing or privileging partnerships and instead rely on traditional collective bargaining and threatening employers with resistance. In their view, it is highly probable that by engaging in partnerships with employers, unions will be co-opted to accept managerial objectives, as in Lukes' (2005) third face of power. Union independence will dissipate and workers' power will weaken longer-term. In contrast, others argue that against a background of declining union membership, extended partnership between employers and unions can support union survival rather than employer anti-union tactics (Ackers and Payne, 1998; Johnstone and Wilkinson, 2018; Teague and Donaghey, 2009).

Yet, another group of authors take a more cautious view of alleged union power gains from partnership (Dobbins and Dundon, 2017; Kochan et al., 2008). On the one hand, they appreciate potential partnership benefits, for example unions and employers actively participating in social dialogue to beget enhanced decision-making benefiting workers. However, it is also argued that union–management partnerships are often fragile and outcomes can lack sufficient power to challenge austerity or managerially imposed changes. As Batt (2018) explains, investor capitalism does not incentivise owners to establish co-operative stakeholder relations (e.g. with unions or employees). From this perspective, power and influence through partnership is only likely to emerge when competitive strategies revolve around quality, skill and innovation, rather than cost (Bélanger and Edwards, 2007; Dobbins and Gunnigle, 2009). Furthermore, in voluntarist industrial relations systems with loose regulation that discourages risk-taking, even if managers and unions support co-operative collaboration, meaningful collaboration is rare (Martínez Lucio and Stuart, 2005; Simms *et al.*, 2012). That is to say, achieving an equitable long-lasting balance of voice and equality is difficult without extensive legislation to constrain employer power (Dobbins and Dundon, 2017). Missing in much of the partnership narrative is the importance of worker rights and independent representation – as seen with the works councils debate above, otherwise risks to unions are high and problematic, especially where union de-recognition or marginalisation is a reality (Martínez Lucio and Stuart, 2005). Alongside and/or operating differently to partnership is collective bargaining as a source of influence and power, discussed next.

Collective bargaining

Of all worker voice types, collective bargaining is perhaps most extensive in terms of its capacity to influence employer actions and decisions. It is a process of negotiation between worker (union) representatives and employers, at sector, industry or workplace levels. It serves at least three specific power and influence functions: *economic*, *governmental* and *decision-making* (Chamberlain and Kuhn, 1965). The *economic* function is about redistributing and sharing wealth created by labour, by negotiating pay and other worker benefits. Equally, the economic function provides a level playing field for all firms in an industry, and thereby restricts unscrupulous employers from paying low wages. The *governmental* function underscores that collective bargaining is a political and power-centred process. Workers and managers are mutually dependent on each other, and through collective bargaining, union representatives can veto, block or support proposed management changes that apply across sectors and industries. This leads to the third function, that of *decision-making*, which allows workers (through their elected union negotiators) to play a part in jointly deciding the rules of the game management set.

Collective bargaining is not an exclusive management system but relies on both sides contributing to how it operates in good faith. In theory, collective bargaining has been argued to be an extremely practical form of industrial democracy (Clegg, 1972), with variable coverage in different countries and across different workplace enterprises (Grady and Simms, 2018). The positive impacts from bargaining is visible when trade unions influenced government policy during the initial response to COVID-19. In the UK, for example, the TUC directly influenced the Chancellor of the Exchequer to introduce a 80 per cent pay subsidy to protect furloughed workers (Novak, 2020). In Austria and Denmark, a more established system of tripartite bargaining between the government, unions and employer associations was central to worker protections (Collington, 2020). In the United States also, health care unions saved lives by battling for personal protective equipment for workers in New York City (Featherstone, 2020).

Significantly, the evidence shows a strong equalising effect from coordinated sectoral level collective bargaining (see Figure 4.1). Importantly, greater collective bargaining coverage for workers, links to lower societal inequalities in cross-country data sets. For example, in Figure 4.1, collective bargaining coverage is low in countries such as the United States, Turkey, Costa Rica, Korea (less than or around 10 per cent bargaining coverage), and in these cases inequality ratios are some of the highest in the world. Conversely, in countries with relatively higher collective bargaining coverage in Figure 4.1 (e.g. Belgium, Finland, Sweden), societal inequality ratios are among the lowest in the world. In other words, collective bargaining through trade unions has a positive social and economic redistributive effect for society as a whole. Grimshaw and Hayter (2020: 160) argue:

> Higher coverage by collective agreements is also associated with a lower gender pay gap. Collective agreements raise the wage floor and thus the relative pay of women who tend to be over-represented at the bottom of the wage distribution.

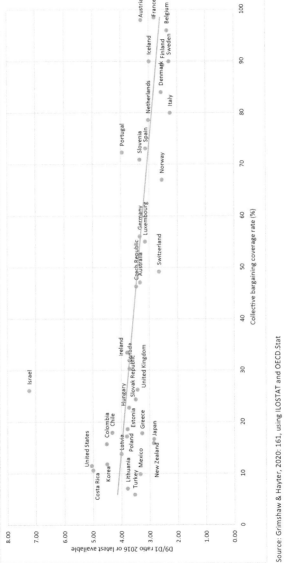

Source: Grimshaw & Hayter, 2020: 161, using ILOSTAT and OECD.Stat.

Figure 4.1 Equality/inequality ratios (D9/D1) and collective bargaining coverage (2016 or latest available)

In summary, trade unions remain extremely important to uplift workers' terms and conditions. The state is important here. A recent initiative of note is the Fair Work Wales Commission (2019), in which the government seeks to legislate for worker participation rights through a Social Partnership Act. Importantly, it promotes collective bargaining as protecting legitimate and socially responsible employers from other, less scrupulous businesses. Thus, while union membership has experienced decline, often owing to global neoliberal economic models that actively seek to weaken union power as well as reduce the role of other voice institutions, evidence and policy preferences demonstrate substantial gains for workers and society from collective bargaining. For workers who have access to union representation and are covered by collective bargaining, protections are certainly more robust than those workers who are unorganised. It is to non-union forms of workers voice we turn next, considering tactics of union avoidance imposed by some employers.

Non-union voice and union-avoidance

A further issue is who speaks for those workers who cannot avail union representation or collective bargaining at a workplace? This calls into question a range of non-union mechanisms and practices that, at surface level, may signal a form of power exercised by employers to deter workers from organising (Gall and Dundon, 2013). The typical channels for non-union voice include things like non-union employee representation committees, similar to JCCs but without union shop stewards. Other methods are individualised and include quality circles, speak-up programmes, suggestion schemes and team briefings to workers by a manager. Non-union voice can be a subtle form of union avoidance, reflecting Lukes' (2005) third face of power, which is not always obvious or openly hostile and aggressive. An example can be witnessed in the highly acclaimed Netflix film, *American Factory*.[2] It is a true story of a Chinese company, Fuyao, who take over a failing car window screen manufacture in Dayton, Ohio. In one scene the CEO and Chairman is openly furious because workers want union representation, to which he threatens to 'shut the factory down' if a union is recognised. Workers encounter unsafe conditions; some are seen with physical burns and injuries from glass furnaces, and many feel their pay is far too low for the sector and jobs they do. It is subsequently reported that Fuyao spends around US$1 million on the services of an anti-union consultant to support the company to defeat a union certification campaign. These union-busting consultants represent a multi-billion dollar industry globally and seek to present a face of non-unionism as legitimate, when in fact it is highly dubious (Gall and Dundon, 2013; Logan, 2013). It also symbolises a power resource for corporations that unions and workers simply cannot afford to match, at least not financially. Rather than describe all possible non-union voice channels, we focus on one particular overarching employer strategy which has distinct anti-union power features: 'double breasting voice', also referred to as 'dual-shop arrangements' (Wilkinson *et al.*, 2020).

The double-breasting concept originated in the US construction sector and was designed purposely to divide workers in the same organisation who would compete for jobs and contracts (Lipsky and Farber, 1976). Double-breasting is an arrangement where a company has union bargaining at one plant or location, while simultaneously operating a non-union consultative arrangement at another plant or location. Thus, some workers have access to union-based channels, while other employees in the same company, but at a different location, only have access to non-union voice mechanisms. The objective is that non-union employees may undermine union bargaining during pay and contract negotiations. 'Double breasting' has been reported as a growing pattern to undermine union power across different countries; for example in Australia (Bamber *et al.*, 2009), America (Verma and Kochan, 1985), Ireland (Lavelle *et al.*, 2010), Canada (Rose, 1986) and the UK (Beaumont and Harris, 1992). Similar anti-union sentiment by governments and employers can be found affecting millions of workers across the global south too; in Colombia (Blackburn and Puerto, 2013), South Korea (Rowley and Bae, 2013) and Indonesia (Ford, 2013).

At workplace level, Dundon *et al.* (2014a) report on double-breasting tactics used to undermine worker power in four separate case study organisations. In one organisation, known as BritCo, employees in Northern Ireland had access to union arrangements, while BritCo workers in the Republic of Ireland did not. These authors show that employer motives for double-breasting can be complex. They propose a 'spill over effect' thesis, arguing that double-breasting outcomes are likely to result in conflict and tension rather than any embedded commitment among the non-union section. In other words, when workers are denied a legitimate union voice, employees soon realise that the system is unfair, yet may fear organising against management without the institutions to support the collective solidary described by Doellgast *et al.* (2018) in Chapter 1 to challenge anti-union employer strategies.

Of course, recruiting union members is difficult not only when faced with anti-union management plans, but also because of other factors such as job demands or the particular role of the nation state. On the one hand, workers employed on low wages and temporary contracts may feel they cannot afford union membership. Others may 'free ride' – that is take the benefits of union bargaining, but not join as individuals. More realistically, however, is many workers in non-union firms may perceive union membership a job security risk, because their employer may be hostile towards unions. Such a culture is also underpinned by government. For example, the UK Trade Union Act (2016) enforces a 50 per cent participation threshold for unions organising strike action (Darlington and Dobson, 2015). This threshold is difficult to meet among standard contract employees, let alone vulnerable precarious workers who are often widely dispersed.

Union organising and counter-mobilising

In response to employer anti-unionism, alternative union and work organising approaches have emerged to leverage better worker influence. Key factors affecting union capacity building are, as already noted, the role of the state and whether governments support or resist unionisation and collective values, the nature of the labour market, internal union politics and structures for democracy, and management styles (Alberti *et al.*, 2013; Martínez Lucio *et al.*, 2017). A key challenge in contemporary times is how unions can build solidarity and unity in diversity and across increasingly fragmented job markets (Connolly *et al.*, 2019; Martínez Lucio *et al.*, 2017).

Unions could learn from diverse mobilising tactics and campaigns used to reach workers who are difficult to organise, either because of geographical disparity, anti-union employer attitudes or limited organising resources. For example, in America, an app called 'Work-it' is utilised to recruit union members in the aggressive anti-union company 'Walmart'. 'Work-it' is part of the wider 'Our Walmart' campaign, founded by the United Food and Commercial Workers union. The app enables workers to express grievances about their employment relationship digitally, connect with co-workers in other Walmart branches and become more involved in the organising campaign. Given its success, 'Work-it' is being integrated into other union projects in Australia and the United States. Additionally, the largest channel used by the 'Our Walmart' campaign is grassroots originated Facebook groups. Such groups are used to attract new members, promote the campaign and unite workers across branches (TUC Digital, 2019). Other research has also identified how social media is a potential union tool to build solidarity during disputes (Greene *et al.*, 2003; Hodder and Houghton, 2015). These are new dimensions that can leverage the mobilising power of unions as a force for progressive change (Kelly, 1998).

In terms of the use of new forms of technology as well, the UK TUC has developed a 'Work Smart' app to help workers identify collective strengths and progress in their career, educate workers about workplace rights and advise workers on how to tackle work problems they are experiencing (Worksmart, 2018). There is scope and potential to integrate the 'Work Smart' app into broader organising campaigns to help mobilise other precarious workers and connect to other civil society associations with an advocacy role supporting workers. The latter are newer industrial relations actors, located beyond the immediate work space context, yet at the same time build organising capacity via network agency, which we turn to consider next.

Voices beyond the workplace

The discussion about who speaks for whom on work and employment matters suggests we need to know more about political spaces beyond the workplace. In particular, there are a whole range of intermediary groups and co-operative bodies who are sympathetic to equality and justice in society, and some have long reached out as formal partners and/or informal coalitions with trade unions (Heery *et al.*, 2012a; MacKenzie and Martínez Lucio, 2005). For instance, co-operatives have different ownership structures to typical hierarchical, profit-driven capitalist organisations, because workers may jointly own the enterprise. This can provide workers with higher levels of power and influence over decision making and working conditions. In some cases, co-operatives are established to challenge profit-driven organisations and tend to leverage better voice arrangements for workers. An example is Fairmondo, a global online platform owned by its users and selling ethical products challenges large online retailers such as Amazon (Howcroft and Bergvall-Kåreborn, 2019). The Coop Cycle platform enables gig-economy workers to manage their deliveries (Lenaerts *et al.*, 2018). However, power-sharing in co-operatives may still be constrained by internal politics and the market pressures such enterprises experience.

In addition to worker co-operative type bodies, other groups with potential to affect voice and power issues at work are CSOs and non-government organisations (NGOs). Such external agencies are not homogenous, and we briefly highlight four types ('external support' bodies; 'interest-based representation' organisations; 'mobilising social movements'; and 'network oriented' agents). After reviewing these different external actor types, we discuss some 'challenges and problems' with such types in the context of worker power and influence.

External support bodies and their influence

External advisory organisations such as the Citizens Advice Bureau provide information to assist employees with workplace relations issues, such as dismissal, pay discrimination and working hours (Pollert, 2010). Legal advice centres provided by local authorities or other CSOs offer employee advice and assist with employment law matters. Holgate *et al.*'s (2012) study looked at Kurdish advice centres with local networks, showing that community knowledge helps build trust and share knowledge within a demographic that might not otherwise have access to traditional worker representation or union bargaining.

However, many local advisory centres are under severe financial pressures, limiting their capacity to meet the demand for individual support (Tailby *et al.*, 2011). For other similar agencies, such as Unemployed Workers' Centres, their remit to support workers has narrowed since the 1980s because of funding and resource constraints. To this end, capacity to influence wider worker populations may be narrow or confined to small pockets of specific advisory influence. Nonetheless, given union decline and absence in many workplaces, the quality of support and influence has been impactful for those workers concerned who would otherwise have had no voice. Studies have uncovered their role in developing basic skills and confidence-building that support marginalised workers who go on to contribute positively in the job market (Perrett and Martínez Lucio, 2008; Perrett *et al.*, 2012). Independent and more progressive employment agencies may also develop such roles with greater formal capacity to influence marginalised workers' lives (Forde and MacKenzie, 2010).

Interest-based representation organisations

Interest-based representative labour market organisations are often supportive yet independent of trade unions. They may lobby in their own right or create alliances with other groups over specific issues and campaigns (Heery *et al.*, 2012b). UK examples include: Age UK (dealing with older worker issues); the Fawcett Society (dealing with women's rights/gender pay); Carers UK (providing support and advice to employed/unemployed carers); and Stonewall (dealing with the lobbying and consultation of LGBTQ+ rights). There are also many nationally co-ordinated organisations involved with black and minority ethnic issues, for example Voice for Change England (Perrett and Martínez Lucio, 2009). In other countries, for example Ireland, a community and voluntary pillar group that was previously part of the corporatist social partnership model of industrial relations with the state, represents the voices of older and young people, women, disabled workers, the unemployed, and others (Carney *et al.*, 2012). Internationally, NGOs have been key to raising a range of issues such as sex work and human trafficking

(Frame, 2017). Hence such bodies form an extended agency network capable of influence throughout many national contexts.

Mobilising social movements and new forms of worker voice

Some organisations add an agitation-based or mobilising element to their lobbying and campaign agendas around work and employment concerns. London Citizens/Citizens UK have adopted many of the classic mobilising and social features of the worker movement, leading campaigns around the 'dignity of work' and 'living wages', working closely with academics and other social groups. In the United States the emergence of worker centres that are locally based and not always aligned to trade unions but other social movements are an important development (Fine, 2006). However, these new forms of organisation may, on occasion, link to or may often be in alliance with trade unions, promoting a broader collective mobilisation reaching beyond the workplace (Wills, 2012). Indeed, new forms of small-scale independent worker representation – increasingly new trade unions and not just loose networks – have emerged from some of these struggles. Gig economy workers, for example, have created the first organic and bottom-up trade union in over a century, the Independent Workers' Union of Great Britain (IWGB) and United Voices of the World (UVW), which refrained from aligning with formal federal union governance systems. These represent an attempt to organise 'from below' in new ways and to see collective conflict through more inclusive cultural activities that support collective identity (Peró, 2019).

Network-oriented agents

CSO power to influence work and employment conditions depends on, among other things, the level of networking and forms of new organising engagement. Many CSOs are formalised, with specific bureaucratic structures and roles, often dependent on various forms of funding from members, employers or the nation state. Yet networking helps create informal advocacy to leverage support and a power dynamic to persuade opinion. New organisational forms within work and employment are a growing part of policy-making processes, with many also evaluating companies and public sector employers. Networking generates new possibilities for connecting ideas, sharing information and power resources. Engaging with universities and the learning sector more widely is a recent related development. These networks create large learning and research communities, as funders and research entities in their own right, contributing to knowledge transfer. Research on networking power and politics has looked at how informal worker networks within companies exchange information, both within and across borders (Whittall *et al.*, 2009); how they facilitate social mobilising (Darlington, 2002); how they counter marginalisation of employee groups on the fringe of the formal economy; and how they provide new pathways to help change organisational and job market outcomes. In some cases, informal network groups have supported LGBTQ+ workers relocated to international environments known to be hostile to gay and lesbian values (McNulty *et al.*, 2018).

New forms of networking are also emerging as de facto trade unions such as the IWGB and the UVW, tackling discrimination and precarious work in specific sectors and the gig economy. In Spain, such networks and new unionism forms have been emerging for some time, filling representative gaps left by some larger and more established unions (Alberti and Però, 2018). In Japan, new forms of network-based groups for temporary workers exist (Stewart, 2006). Such developments use networking as a tactic to connect campaigns across people, often with more open and politically led structures (Alberti and Però, 2018). Many are social community networks organised around younger or migrant worker groups, pioneering new forms of mobilisation and campaigning against intransigent employers (Connolly *et al.*, 2019).

A relatively new and continuously developing form of network-orientated power and influence is social media, providing a vehicle for representing specific issues and needs (Hodder, 2014), particularly in relation to younger people. Studies pinpoint how social media can facilitate collective mobilisation (Greene *et al.*, 2003), provide new information channels and support vulnerable migrant workers (Fitzgerald *et al.*, 2012), and even modernise and assist responses to broader organisational change patterns (Martínez Lucio *et al.*, 2009).

Voice from beyond the workplace: engagement, influences and challenges

A key issue is how important and impactful are these bodies in advancing the voice of workers? It is evident that the way external actor groups engage with companies can leverage positive influence for some workers. For example, Citizens UK launched the Living Wage Campaign, which has secured over £210 million in wage increases thus far (Citizens UK, 2017). Furthermore, a Just Equal Treatment campaign in 2007 by Age UK has supported thousands of workers over 65 who would otherwise have been forced out of the job market (Age UK, 2017). Public Concern at Work supports whistle-blowers and helped establish the 'First 100' campaign in 2014, encouraging companies to sign up to a statutory whistleblowing code of practice. This code can be utilised by courts and tribunals; 40 organisations have currently signed up (PCAW, 2017).

There are other intermediary bodies, such as Stonewall in the UK, emphasising the value LGBTQ+ employees bring to the workplace (Stonewall, 2017a); or the CIPD, which holds a 'People Management Award' annually, to recognise organisations based on their inclusive and equitable people management and employee learning initiatives; and the Involvement and Participation Association, which advises on and promotes forms of industrial democracy in industry.

Fundamental is how external bodies link with and influence governance systems, for example rights-based networks such as women's sections or black worker committees within companies and trade unions. Research has outlined how they impact internal agendas, trade union priorities and the development of specific representation forms (Kirton and Healy, 2012; McBride, 2002). A range of studies explore the development of black worker sections within trade unions (Virdee and Grint, 1994), along with focused campaigns and forms of organisation linked to the changing nature of migration (Fitzgerald and Hardy, 2010). Distinct forms of organisation and various strategies have evolved to ensure the voice of more vulnerable workers within trade unions, although whether these have re-addressed various social and political imbalances is uncertain. However, such initiatives have notably shifted union agendas and policies over time. Several gaps remain in terms of the consistency of influence internally from various black and minority ethnic groups (Martínez Lucio and Perrett, 2009), the extent of direct involvement within worker representation (Connolly *et al.*, 2014b), and campaigns that extend worker voices beyond a workplace (McBride and Greenwood, 2009). Moreover, the politics of such networks and their legitimacy is important to the way they develop new forms of voice and influence, although there are issues and challenges to consider.

One issue is the possible crowding-out and competition between such bodies which may affect their ability to shape voice related matters. Tensions may arise between some unions and the living wage campaigns, or between groups covering similar topics and interests (Connolly *et al.*, 2019; see Heery *et al.* 2012b for a discussion of trade union relations with CSOs). There is a notable difference between Stonewall, with its more corporate and market facing approach, and the Peter Tatchell Foundation, which is more focused on mobilisation and has a more left-leaning political approach to LGBTQ+ issues. Funding for such bodies can also be uneven and there may be extensive competition between them for limited private and public funds as the state withdraws support for NGOs and related bodies. Complexity can create broad but fragmented employee representation and support institutional frameworks that may exacerbate competition and political distrust. One major problem may be that the perceived need for voice at work is removed in some cases, as companies seek accreditation on the living wage, equality management and health and safety issues through such external organisations (e.g. the Living Wage Foundation in the UK, Stonewall, and wellbeing based consultancies). Hence, companies may use some of these external bodies to constrain worker voice, which may result in a bypassing of collective representation at a workplace.

Conclusion

It is evident when considering 'who speaks for workers' that power and politics matter in promoting and weakening worker voice. If workers in a country or industry enjoy institutional and legally supported collective bargaining, then they will probably experience less inequality and discrimination than those who labour under non-union regimes or voluntary consultation committees. However, these institutional mechanisms need to be underpinned by robust and independent worker organisations and networks of worker activists. Indeed, these networks and actors are evolving in form and style, which to some extent fragment in both negative and positive ways. For these reasons, worker voice is highly politicised and a complex space for competing organisations and networks.

Arguably, effective voice and worker representation is a necessary conduit underpinning human rights to counter the worst excesses of managerial power and investor-led capitalism (Thompson, 2003). As Hyman (2015a: 12) argues, it is incompatible to be a free citizen (e.g. vote in elections) but be denied a voice in the workplace. The very idea of contributing to society cannot be separated from the right to have a say about work and employment matters inside the office or factory, and these matters affect the future of work, discussed next in Chapter 5.

Notes

1 www.ipa-involve.com/faqs/a-guide-to-the-information-and-consultation-of-employees-regulations [accessed 12 February 2020].
2 www.youtube.com/watch?v=m36QeKOJ2Fc [accessed 15 January 2020].

5
Work and future contexts

Introduction

The analysis in this book has been informed by six dimensions that can influence work and employment issues, first summarised in Chapter 1 (Table 1.1). These dimensions include: (1) labour indeterminacy and structured antagonism outlined in Chapter 1; (2) management actions, labour market utilisation and new technologies, discussed in Chapter 2; (3) globalisation, also debated in Chapter 2; (4) the role of the state and employment regulation, examined in Chapter 3; (5) the communication sphere covered in Chapter 4 on worker voice; and (6), the future of work contexts, as reviewed in this final chapter.

In this chapter we review three broad future developments concerned with trajectories of power and influence at work. Importantly, trying to map the future and competing developments is not navel-gazing or blind crystal ball predictions, but rather informed by the relevance of attendant conditions and relationship dynamics: for example, the particular social context of work (e.g. gig economy; manufacturing or skilled trades); the power of the nation state and employment regulation; and/or the way employers utilise labour and implement strategic choices (e.g. market performance measures, quality service or adopt union avoidance plans). Future developments are not static models – or binary ones – but broad continua with overlapping and evolving contexts and issues. In a key contribution, Richard Hyman (2015b) provided an analysis of how working conditions deteriorate further with a constant unravelling of the social consensus built during the twentieth century. He contrasted this scenario with two sets of alternative scenarios that could, to some extent, counter these more negative outcomes. One was an 'elite project', where the state and various social elites try to stem the corrosion of economic and social conditions by establishing various standards and codes of conduct, led by organisations such as the United Nations and the ILO. Alternatively, there is the possibility – and in some cases reality – of a much stronger politics and counter movement that may emerge through a more 'confrontational approach', by questioning the basic premise of socio-economic power structures. However, we try to nuance such a view by mapping three future developments, each shaped by different sets of contextual circumstances and factors. The future is likely to see a greater set of parallel realities running alongside each other (even, perhaps, in the context of worsening conditions overall).

The first we label a *reinvigorated minimalist state*, which mirrors one part of Hyman's intervention. Here the state (and related state agencies and bodies) address a burgeoning void of citizen (worker) rights, which may find a new space in post-Brexit and/or post-COVID landscape, either as deregulated or moderated protectionism, akin to some elements outlined by Howell (2005) when discussing individual rights. The nature of the state's role has some resonance with French and Raven (1959) in terms of expert power and the use of a broader set of relations and referent points.

We differentiate this from a second potential future development that covers a spectrum of *soft re-regulation and increasingly voluntary social dialogue*. In this future, private and semi-public agencies offer expert advice on key employment issues, such as new homeworking arrangements after COVID or gig economy contracts (e.g. by state conciliation bodies such as the Advisory, Conciliation and Arbitration Service (ACAS) in the UK, private research and consultancy based organisations such as the Resolution Foundation or Royal Society for the Arts, and pseudo-government commissions such as UK's Taylor Review of Modern Working Practices). This development opens up space for manipulation by employer-led consultancies and/or employer associations.

The third future development includes the formation of new 'collective alliances and coalition-building' among a range of social actors, with organised labour remaining pivotal in some respects but varying in its role. We may witness enhanced political awareness among labour market activists, who seek to promote harder employment regulations, and newer demands to value those workers who kept society functioning during the COVID pandemic (e.g. care workers, shop assistants, delivery drivers, etc.). It may transpire that the progressive role of the state is spurred on by a growing political consciousness influenced by global standards for basic rights. This development is not a return to some imagined golden age of labourism, but a hybrid of alliances forming new and potentially diverse collective opportunities for (strong) workplace solidarities for voice, both inside but also increasingly beyond the workplace sphere among community coalitions.

In this respect, it is important to break down the three developments further as they provide worker representatives and organisations with a more complex set of reference points that are different and may need various response strategies of balance or emphasis. It is important that we manage to unpick the different nuances and politics of a move away from a neoliberal or de-regulation perspective as there will be different possibilities and challenges for workers as they navigate a more complex and fragmented terrain. Before discussing the three broad developments and trajectories, let us first outline and recap the current landscape with regard to the nature of employment relations power, politics and influence.

Contemporary challenges: fragmented and fractured power relations

It is evident that worker voice has diminished considerably over recent decades. Not only has union membership and collective bargaining coverage declined substantially, but other aspects have also worsened. For example, the rights that do exist for workers – say health and safety, parental leave or rights in the communication sphere for information and consultation – are increasingly individualised. The latter means workers have had to articulate and argue for their rights as individuals, which renders their position in the employment relationship more precarious and subject to management prerogative.

Reviewing contemporary debates may paint a picture that things are getting worse. It can be argued that opportunities for voice and influence are increasingly fragmented and fractured, where certain factors 'combine' to weaken workplace power and influence. For example, factors reviewed in Chapter 2, including the outsourcing of jobs and the deployment of new technologies, 'combine' with other dimensions which then weaken the position of labour in the relationship. Evidence in Chapter 3 shows such 'combining' factors include bogus self-employed contracts, which lead to greater precarity for many workers in newer sectors such as the gig economy, but also for those in more established labour markets for education and health care. Workers here face insecure and temporary employment or, worse still, are defined as self-employed when the reality is they are a worker in any meaningful sense of the word, who is subject to considerable employer control over work allocation and prescribed job tasks.

The pattern of fragmenting worker voice is further evidenced through what appear to be 'evasive' employer tactics. Evidence discussed in Chapter 4 reported a decoupling of institutional supports for voice (e.g. works councils, JCCs) through the use of double-breasting voice and union avoidance tactics, which actively seek to pitch one group of workers against another group. Non-union voice as a whole was found to be considerably weaker when compared with unionised collective bargaining, not only at organisational level but also with spill-over consequences for societal inequalities, where countries with low collective bargaining coverage are considerably more unequal (Grimshaw and Hayter, 2019; Chapter 4). This goes some way towards explaining why many employers and some governments remain actively hostile to trade union bargaining, and redesign legal enactment to weaken collective power, such as the Trade Union Act 2016 in the UK to restrict trade union actions (Grady and Simms, 2018).

Overall, the extent of 'fragmented' and 'fractured' power relations raises contemporary debates about the desirable forms of corporate governance. As seen in Chapter 2, it raises questions about the negative impact of globalisation on labour rights around the world. Issues of work flexibility are increasingly misguided, by placing value on how goods determined by market attraction are priced (e.g. for necessary lifesaving drugs by pharmaceutical corporations), rather than the factors that go into making the product and its value that has distributive outcomes beyond corporate profit maximisation (Mazzucato, 2019). Value capture and extraction is indicative of the experiences of work intensification encountered by workers around the globe. Importantly, what counts as value is almost always predicated on flexibility 'of' the worker (effort, time, hours, pay), and flexibility driven 'for' the value of firm (Proctor, 2006). The labour market debates in Chapter 2 connect to concerns as to how far (or to what extent) the state is able and willing to support its citizens with labour market protections, as evidenced through COVID wage subsidiary schemes by different countries and governments. As discussed in Chapter 3, the state has filled a vacuum on occasions to support workers because of growing inequalities and a gap in social and economic protections, but it has also been unwilling for political and ideological reasons to legislate for more mandatory universal rights or support statutory collective bargaining in many liberalised economies. There are, therefore, questions about who is speaking up for whom, as discussed in Chapter 4.

These contemporary challenges resulting in a weaker and fragmented labour agency are not static or wholly pessimistic. For example, while worker voice has diminished over space and time, there are nonetheless pockets of renewed engagement that signals not only a degree of continuity, but also structures of workforce change led by reinvigorated social networks and more radical work and employment research approaches, some of which will be summarised next.

Three future potential developments in work

In this book we have aimed to locate our analysis of worker influence within a broader perspective of WES, connecting with sociological and political debates in the field. In doing so, we have reviewed the contours and contexts that shape the sources of power, the resources affecting mobilisation, and the conduits for workers to express their voices across a range of dimensions. As others have suggested, we cannot simply accept a pessimistic view that heralds a fundamental decline in the collective influence of worker power (D'Art and Turner, 2002). While the decline in worker voice and the ascendency of power towards capital can at times appear all-encompassing, it is in fact only part of the story, and there are more subtle nuances and uneven pockets of counter-mobilisation that are important in shaping the nature and future of work.

The tendency among academics to engage with futurology is fraught with problems and if anything is certain it is that predicting any future outcome is unwise. Despite the joyful extrapolations of leading Massachusetts Institute of Technology, Oxbridge and other better-known scholars or editors of the quality press, expectations that technology will replace all our jobs in the future is often over-exaggerated bunkum. The reality is we are unlikely to see robotics or artificial intelligence freeing people from the hardship of labour degradation, while employers around the globe continue to rely on paying people very low wages. Nevertheless, the questions about power, voice and influences at work are likely to be more complex and decoupled from established structures of governance in the future. The manner in which demands will be represented and interests defended will be of growing importance to multiple actors. One question is how competing representations will coexist, combine and/or vary. Another question is whether new demands will serve conflicting, or shared labour market interests. Beyond the ongoing fragmentation of worker influence – which we question in terms of it being some kind of inevitability – there are various ways these complex spaces will develop and evolve.

There is always the reality that things are pretty undesirable for most people who have to work to sustain a living. And it may be likely that things will just get worse. Backed by a toothless regulatory state, corporations may continue to exploit new technologies and artificial intelligence simply for their own gain, without recognising the potential for wider societal value from such innovations, thereby simultaneously making people's jobs more insecure. But rather than repeat the overly pessimistic worldview, in this section we instead chart three possible future developments: (1) a reinvigorated (yet minimalist) state; (2) soft re-regulation and voluntary social dialogue; and (3) collective alliance and coalition building.

A reinvigorated but minimalist state role

A first potential future development may include various contexts that relate to a possible *reinvigorated minimalist state role* for worker voice and influence. On the one hand, the state may seek to enshrine rights, such as individual protections or new laws as employers map out the realities of work in a post-COVID future. On the other hand, the state may elect not to forcibly mandate corporations for improved worker rights, but rather seek to persuade social actors of the moral good and moral economic value in advancing a new 'social contract' between managers and workers. The aim might be to encourage the parties themselves to correct the huge inequalities and negative developments in work and employment that have become endemic over the last few decades, noted in the debates outlined in Chapters 2 and 3. For all the politics and fanfare associated with de-regulation and marketisation, there remain concerns with the greater level of social and labour market fragmentation that have had real effects on workers and their families and there are signals the state may want to redress the uneven playing field, at least to some extent.

In Chapter 3 we saw how the state weakened rights that under-mined vulnerable groups of workers, yet at the same time it also intervened to mitigate some of these developments through the establishment of protections and legal interventions (e.g. regarding sham employment contracts or a lack of personal protective equipment during COVID working). Rubery (2011) has argued that the state cannot escape the consequences of its own labour market with-drawal, and as such needs to re-intervene at key points to allevi-ate – if only minimally – the destructive trail of neoliberal reform (Martínez Lucio, 2018). It could be argued, therefore, that because of diminished worker voice as social agency continues to flounder, the state has had to step in to fill the spaces left by growing labour market inequalities, by setting some basic minimum standard, as with the case of a living wage or temporary COVID wage subsidy scheme. Indeed, it may be witnessed that the state has had to start propagating 'codes of conduct' regarding how employers should behave. It has had to deploy a range of agencies at its disposal to reimagine models and issue codes on voice and areas of employ-ment equality; for example, codes to regulate employer behav-iours promoted publicly by the likes of the Equality and Human Rights Commission, ACAS, or the Health and Safety Commission on stress management and worker wellbeing (Martínez Lucio and Stuart, 2011).

What we may imagine under the first development is a reinvigor-ated state seeking minimal arrangements to support voice and labour market rights. The expansion of new technologies and artificial intelligence shaping the future of work may represent one space that the state could seek to intervene; for example, to improve insecure and ambiguous legal contract standards that have plagued many workers in the gig economy. Some employers may embrace such change, seeing it as a minimally tolerable constraint on management choice, while enabling managers to defend or advance their own interests. Others, even when in the context of substantial changes in the labour market, may not favour the interests of workers or unions; then the state increasingly feels compelled to persuade employers and other agencies to create some semblance of fairness and justice. The argument is that while some positive protections and opportunities to influence worker concerns can be evidenced, these remain subject to employer power to support such offerings, with the state's role confined to a policy channel rather than enforcer of rules. A *reinvigorated but minimal state role* is more likely to consolidate employer influence and leave workers undermined or, at best, comparatively weaker as a collective agency relative to the power of markets and corporate bosses.

Soft (re)regulation and broader voluntary social dialogue

The second development may include 'positive' trajectories, which promote various *softer forms of regulation and voluntary social dialogue*. The nature and changing role of the state is again central and may fluctuate between the champion for voluntary policy options combined with other mandatory protections. Here we may see some of the broader global and geo-political forces having relevance on work and employment change, including responses to climate challenges where workers are employed in fossil fuel industries or other environmentally damaging sectors. The COVID-19 crisis initiated a somewhat more reinvigorated role for the state in supporting workers facing layoffs and loss of earnings, but the timing and nature of government interventions varied across countries (Collington, 2020; TUC, 2020).

At a general level, the role of the state has been mixed and highly variable across different countries. On the one hand, state interventions have been constrained and resources depleted since the Second World War era, as discussed in Chapter 2, often due to ideological and political objectives including privatisation and the mission to 'roll back' the frontiers of the state. Governments have actively sought to open up new spaces for private entrepreneurship, which, at the time, meant curbing the collective rights of workers and have added future problems in terms of the environment. On the other hand, some state undertakings (which vary across different countries) have had a substantial legacy on a whole manner of key employment issues, including commissions of inquiry, new research pathways, labour market activation policies, and new developmental and informational activities. All of which result in the state being a pioneer of change: the 'unsung' hero or backbone of many contemporary developments in a range of new technologies and related spaces for job creation (Mazzucato, 2015). In many ways, the same goes for its role in worker and adult education, welfare supports and the core institutional fabric of labour markets, even though these have reduced considerably since the 1980s. The state can design policy options to share and redistribute the gains from new technologies into sectors and jobs that may not avail of a shiny robotic future. For example, health care is often low-paid and undervalued work and/or emerging newer green industry jobs may benefit from state-led supports. Furthermore, with an ageing population and advances in medical treatments, the workforce is working longer and increased numbers of older people will need care in the future. The productive gains from technology in one sector can be shared to recognise and value work in other sectors, such as health and care work, as well as help reduce future climate risks.

To this extent, we may find a more positive situation emerging from the point of view of workers, with the state opening up the spaces for social dialogue and improved work and employment issues, in a way that supports a new social contract with both capital and labour. Regulation is soft in the sense that it is shaped and determined by agencies and actors, rather than being mandated by laws. The risk is that some employers will support and may even champion such an agenda as a way to advance their own interests, while other firms remain disconnected from the social context of work and frustrate the opportunities to engage in affective dialogue with worker representatives. It is likely employers will control the agenda and present an image of inclusion and/or exclusion, shaped by their preferences and power resources. Under these variable predications, the state functions as a reference guide or referee, seeking to shape the rules towards a set of (higher) minimums for better labour market inclusion. The problems are such developments and set of practices present risks for workers who lack the resources, power and systems to challenge obstinate employers (Martínez Lucio and Stuart, 2005).

New collective alliances and coalition networks among a broader range of actors

The third potential future development involves a deepening of active *collective alliance and coalition-building*, albeit with uneven and to some extent unpredictable political pathways: the previous chapter outlined some of the ways the voices of NGO/CSO actors were expanding or multiplying worker interests. To be sure, the contemporary political landscape since the financial crisis of 2008, and further compounded with the COVID-19 economic downturn, have led to greater uncertainty and unpredictability. The very nature and future of worker influence may take alternative extreme pathways, either bolstered by a state-led interest for greater industrial democracy, as some politicians seek to substitute the representative rights that workers may lose as Britain exits the European social market, or there is a race to reform the UK into a low-tax and low-quality job market, to attract foreign direct investment premised on cheap labour, under World Trade Organization free market criteria. Whatever path emerges, the challenges for organised labour and those interested in a progressive social voice, will need to be far-reaching so as to push and steer the debate towards fairness within work, perhaps through a range of direct measures but also multiple informational alliances (Martínez Lucio and MacKenzie, 2017; Martínez Lucio and Stuart, 2011).

The issues affecting worker rights may leverage broader global sustainable standards linked to political developments and networked groups in particular nation states. Examples may be observed in the ILO's 'Future of Work Commission', championing new opportunities to upskill employee capabilities and support more inclusive labour market institutions. Similarly, the UN's 'Sustainability Goals' promote 17 agenda-setting ambitions including, among others, better health and wellbeing, gender equality, decent work, climate action and strong institutions. On these issues the state – for all its declining capacity and increasingly limited reach – is the main agent capable of fundamentally altering the rules of the game by

enacting new laws, repealing older statutes or removing long established rights. Above all, there is space for progressive persuasion and
influence to address issues of fairness and benchmark standards for
decent work: thus, pessimism is not obvious or assured. This pushes
the role of political activity within the industrial relations sphere to
the centre of the agenda and signals a potentially renewed role for
trade unions and other labour market activists to form emerging
progressive coalitions.

Depending on the nature and variability of groups forming social
alliances, this third development could be an emerging trajectory
for new collectivism, where there is a much wider dialogue related
to the meaning of fairness at work. Arguably, any future possibility
cannot evolve without having regard to a range of union types and
various social mobilising agents (e.g. the Living Wage Foundation,
Stonewall for LGBTQ+ issues, Mind for mental health, Oxfam's
work to improve equalities in less developed countries – among others). What is more, within the trade union movement – new and old,
bureaucratic top-down and organic bottom-up – one has to consult
a range of departments dealing with health and safety, vulnerable
workers, equality issues, migrant workers, trade union training and
international affairs (among others). We have seen a multiplicity of
structures emerge to some extent, even within the HRM function in
large corporations, as it changes to cope with and manage diversity
(or close down factories and plants).

The space for newer alliances and collective identities is one that
has potential for unions to mobilise for future influence. Arguably,
coalition-building would be vital around specific issues, and overar-
ching principles, and is a function that trade unions are well versed
in given their longevity of governance structures and democratic
accountability. There could be alliances between types of trade
unions; for example, large traditional trade unions working alongside smaller flexible unions linked to migrant networks, issues of
climate change and homelessness, or marginalised sectors (e.g. gig
economy). There could easily develop collective alliances around
the propagation of the living wage, gender pay equalisation, decent
work, sustainable employment, environmental responsibilities
and other social movement campaigns where civil society organisations (religious or otherwise) and trade unions seek to influence

'progressive' employers to improve working standards (Heery *et al.*, 2017; Wills *et al.*, 2009). Oxfam, for example, has made important upskilling improvements to help empower women workers in partnership with specific multinational corporations across its global supply chain network (Wilshaw *et al.*, 2016).

Important developments in this area include devolved regulation: for example among local authorities in England, Scotland and Wales where there has been a relatively more active agenda to sustain and champion improved working standards and conditions (Stuart *et al.*, 2016). Emerging alliances have been found at local city council level with spill-over effects supporting more focused and devolved forms of regulation, embedded as part of a set of new rules towards upgrading workers' rights across local authority suppliers, as drivers for a new living wage narrative (Johnson, 2017). There are also a range of initiatives where employers and social organisations link up on specific work-related projects, for example Stonewall linking up to provide training or advice for management in their approach to LGBTQ+ communities in their workplace. Within this context is the importance of collective activities from seeking alliances and setting common and progressive work-related agendas: creating alternative forms of language and common principles is essential. In such a situation, the informational and strategic capacity of worker representatives and leaders within trade unions will be pivotal as they learn to navigate a very broad set of social and private organisations – and interests – against an uncertain political future. At the same time, of course, HR managers and employer associations will no doubt be forming their own alliances.

The use of new technologies and digital platforms for social media and labour activism can be crucial here: it is often through social media that work-related campaigns find their way through to the public at large and through which organisational structures of a more flexible and inclusive nature are developed. The role of the internet has been the subject of debate within the discipline of industrial relations for over 20 years (Geelan and Hodder, 2017; Lee, 1997). Unions have advanced in terms of ICT for engaging members and promoting worker voices, although much depends on the context in which people work and the skills needed to access technology. Homeworking and the use of technology raised its head as a major issue during the COVID-19 crisis, and many workers had no choice but to adapt their homes to continue working as best as possible. In many ways, technology has liberated but also brought new work stresses and anxieties because of the switch to home-working during COVID-19 response measures. Whether workers are adequately compensated remains an ongoing debate, and network groups and trade union alliances have pioneered health and safety protections on these issues (Featherstone, 2020). On other matters and campaigns, in the United States labour activists have launched apps, blogs and social media platforms to engage and connect with younger workers; 'co-worker.org' was launched in 2013 (Wood, 2016) and within three years had connected with one in ten Starbucks workers to support worker voice. Likewise, in the UK the TUC has a Digital Lab (Wood, 2019) and connects with related content such as Level-Up (www.welevelup.org/), campaigning to end sexism in the workplace. Other examples include 'iamthecode'; a global movement to empower women and girls to enhance their computing and coding skills to participate in the labour market and eliminate poverty. Thus, the opportunities to expand collective communities and solidarities using advanced new technologies are potentially far-reaching. The capacities within unions and other labour groups to use digital ICT for voice will remain vital for the raising of new concerns at work and in sustaining activism related to them: although management are also using such tools as a form of counter-communication as well, the extent of competition and conflict will increasingly take on new forms. Nevertheless, in this case one can see the need for alliance-building and the logic of coalition as being key to extending worker interests and the better utilisation of artificial intelligence and technology in terms of fairness.

A further variant of a potentially future alliance-building landscape is one where trade unions, as some of the largest non-government organisations in many societies, become pivotal to the spreading of a more inclusive collective mindset in society more broadly. They can communicate the way fairness at work is defined and becomes normalised beyond the immediacy of the workplace. In a similar way to the state, and for all the talk of decline, it is evident that trade unions remain nationally oriented with robust structures of governance who seek justice and equality in a sea of fragmentation. Some progressive political parties have not ruled out a new legal manifesto that will underpin a stronger collective mandatory framework for bargaining and voice (Ewing *et al.*, 2016). For instance, the political response to, and critique of, the neoliberal model has been alive in the political debates emerging from the 15-M protest movements in Spain in terms of Podemos, the phenomena of Bernie Saunders and left and socialist democrats in America, the emergence of a new broader left in the UK, and the role of protests within Latin America against the state or for citizenship rights and broader voice in Hong Kong and China, all pushing the state on matters of a fairer and more inclusive system for work, as well as wider societal equalities. Such a context and framework may create a more level labour market playing field and bolster the role of trade unions through indirect forms of representation and/ or extend influence through a greater series of rights with regards to strikes and political action.

In addition, issues of worker control, industrial democracy and even worker ownership may emerge in a more central manner in this particular context. The question of industrial democracy has returned to the political landscape – rhetorically at least in recent years – not least due to issues of management malpractice and corporate corruption in terms of finance and pension funds (Gold and Waddington, 2019; Gollan and Markey, 2001). Under this third development, the possibility of a more critical and radically democratic dimension may develop – although it need not given the array of actors and interests in terms of NGOs and others as pointed out in Chapter 4. One may see new broader industrial strategy agendas within future of work debates: greater political engagement and mobilisation against the hierarchical nature of the employment relation and the sources of inequity within the current socio–economic system. Within this third development – compared to the previous two – the issue of worker control *may* be promoted as part of a broader political landscape to the issues of labour market fragmentation and social exclusion: although this may be interpreted in various ways and not necessarily in the critical manner suggested by Hyman (2015b).

Of course, it also seems difficult perhaps to envision a future of work determined by greater equalities using robust and legally mandated collective bargaining, extended worker voice and sustainable corporations connecting with an inclusive alliance of networks, underpinned by a statutory floor of rights for all workers. But the image is more the norm to some extent in many countries such as Sweden, Switzerland and Denmark. Indeed, it should be noted, the way trade unions have engaged increasingly with questions of health and safety, equality, justice and broader employment themes and social issues is noticeable and may lead to a greater degree of influence. The way mobilisation takes place and is politicised is one that is premised on creating common causes and attributing responsibility around a range of alliances and processes, with regards to systems of tripartite governance or more broader spaces for alliance-building on worker rights. Indeed, trade unions have not withdrawn from the political landscape but have in some cases been central to the reconfiguration of progressive politics – although whether this will lead to greater and sustainable levels of influence is another matter, such are the contingencies within the realm of the political and related uncertainties due to issues of right-wing populism.

Conclusion

We can be sure that for all our forward thinking – and visions of what could be – reality has a way of never sticking to a certain path. No one can predict the way work will be organised and worker influence structured in some near or distant future. There are no clear future pathways per se but highly contradictory and varied developments that interface with each other in evolving yet fragmented contexts. However, the point of the above is to explain that patterns of power and influence in work and employment relations can evolve and change. Within the French and Raven (1959) model, we know that coercion and harder forms of power may be important, as we can see in some of the developments referred to above. But also, informal relations and expert roles combine to create key points of reference that become more central to the way trade unions and worker networks more broadly can be repositioned in a strategic role in the future; just as the role of the state may be. There will be a need to understand how harder interventions and roles are balanced across strategic alliance-building opportunities in the future. In fact, much might depend on what Lukes (1974) stated: influence, encouragement and persuasion are also mobilised in creating a fairer and just approach to life at work. The nature of contemporary voice will require subtle and political manoeuvring by workers and their organisations or, as Gramsci once argued, 'harder forms of power and mobilisation will require a leadership of minds and a new greater sensibility to representing broader social interests around alliances' (see Buci-Glucksmann, 1980). How these strategies set more democratic agendas and the basic understanding of equality and fairness will be important: what fairness means and how the third dimension of power, as Lukes (1974) calls it, is shaped will be fundamental.

The negative predications of the future, with change high-lighted as some sort of inevitable outcome, for example the decline of trade unions, the individualisation of work, the emergence of a stronger managerial and neoliberal framework is not certain (Hyman, 2015b). However, these are opportunities to think about mapping alternatives as illustrations of more positive, albeit var-ied and complex, future developments for strategic reflection. It is our view that various possible 'future developments' can be shaped and reconfigured with a better understanding of the uneven and at times contradictory social processes affecting power and politics in a workplace. These may sometimes interact and present a 'messier' set of opportunities as workers and unions weave between minimal-ist engagement by the state, adapt to sets of (uneven) social respon-sibilities and emerging private regulation strategies by employers and related bodies, while also competing with social and civil society organisations to promote worker voice. We may never see a return to a single representative model with a uniform structure of voice, although whether it was ever that simple is a matter of opinion, but we do need to start re-mapping the opportunities to influence the future of worker voice in a broader manner across different market settings and within multiple organisational forms. In this respect we do not think there will be clear and precise scenarios with pred-icable outcomes, but a chaotic set of developments around certain future contexts of fairness and dignity at work which have a more complex set of contours and create a need for more nuanced naviga-tional strategies from worker representatives. It is for these reasons, as Doellgast *et al.* (2018) suggest, that new and more flexible but also sustainable forms of solidarity and action will be needed to help address the uncertain twists and turns that lie ahead. Hyman (2015b) was right to emphasise that the choice may be between more statist or elitist (top-down) or more social (bottom-up) approaches; but even within these, different choices have to be made and newer and evolving alliances forged, which will require a greater level of dexterity and risk-taking by organised labour: as well as a greater inclusive and imaginative approach to work and its democratisation (Hyman, 2015a). For this reason, we see the space of renewal or change, even when considering positive progressive possibilities, as being immensely political and diverse in terms of its nature.

The central part of this new navigation and manoeuvring will be to recast what we mean by 'work' and what we mean by 'fairness' and 'decency', to look into how organisations are governed, what their economic priorities are, how these priorities sustain longer-term societal wellbeing, what the state does (and does not do) to support greater social inclusion and where a more genuinely and radically democratic society working at all levels fits into this model.

Employment law cases

Addison Lee Ltd v. *Gascoigne* (2018). *EAT*.

Adkins and Others v. *Lex Autolease Limited* (2017). *Employment Tribunal*. 1 March 2017.

Aslam and Others v. *Uber BV and Others* (2016). *Employment Tribunal*. 28 October 2016. 2017 *EAT*. 2018 *Court of Appeal*.

Autoclenz Ltd v. *Belcher and Others* (2011). *IRLR*. 820.

Boxer v. *Excel Group Ltd* (in liquidation) (2017). *Employment Tribunal*.

Byrne Brothers (Formwork) Ltd v. *Baird* (2002). *IRLR*. 96.

Cotswold Developments Construction Ltd v. *Williams* (2006). *IRLR*. 181.

Dewhurst v. *Citysprint UK Ltd*. (2017). *Employment Tribunal*. 1 May 2017.

Independent Workers' Union of Great Britain (IWGB) v. *RoofFoods t/a Deliveroo* (2017). Central Arbitration Committee, TUR1/985(2016), 14.11.2017.

Jivraj v. *Hashwani* (2011). *IRLR*. 827.

Lange and Others v. *Addison Lee Limited* (2017). *Employment Tribunal*. 2018 *EAT*.

Leyland and others v. *Hermes Parcelnet Ltd*. (2018). *Employment Tribunal*.

Obi v. *Verma and Rice Shack Ltd*. (2017). *Employment Tribunal*.

Pimlico Plumbers Limited and Another v. *Smith* (2018). *UKSC*. 29.

Protectacoat Firthglow Ltd v. *Szilagyi* (2009). *IRLR*. 365.

R (on the Application of Unison) v. *Lord Chancellor* (2017). *UKSC*. 51.

SW Global Resourcing Ltd v. *Docherty and Another* (2012). *IRLR*. 727. *EAT* and (2013) CSIH 72 (Inner House of Court of Session in Scotland).

Young and Woods Ltd v. *West* (1980). *IRLR*. 201.

Bibliography

Ackers, P. (2014). 'Rethinking the employment relationship: a neo-pluralist critique of British industrial relations orthodoxy', *International Journal of Human Resource Management*, 25: 18, 2608–2625.

Ackers, P. and J. Payne (1998). 'British trade unions and social partnership: rhetoric, reality and strategy', *International Journal of Human Resource Management*, 9: 3, 529–550.

Adam, D., J. Purcell and M. Hall (2014). 'Joint consultative committees under the Information and Consultation of Employees Regulations: a WERS analysis', *ACAS Research Paper*, 4, 5–53.

Age UK (2017). Available at: ageuk.org.uk/. [Accessed 28 June 2017].

Alberti, G. (2013). 'Intersectionality, trade unions and precarious work', *The International Journal of Human Resource Management*, 24: 22, 4132–4148.

Alberti, G. and D. Però (2018). 'Migrating industrial relations: migrant workers' initiative within and outside trade unions', *British Journal of Industrial Relations*, 56: 4, 693–715.

Alberti, G., J. Holgate and M. Tapia (2013). 'Organising migrants as workers or as migrant workers? Intersectionality, trade unions and precarious work', *International Journal of Human Resource Management*, 24: 22, 4132–4148.

Alberti, G., I. Bessa, K. Hardy, V. Trappmann and C. Umney (2018). 'In, against and beyond precarity: work in insecure times', *Work Employment & Society*, 32: 3, 447–457.

Alhambra, M. A., B. Ter Haar and A. Kun (2011). 'Soft on the inside, hard on the outside: an analysis of new forms of international labour law', *International Journal of Comparative Labour Law and Industrial Relations*, 27: 4, 337–363.

Almond, P. and M. González Menéndez (2014). 'The changing nature of HRM, organizational change and globalization', in M. Martínez

Lucio (ed.) *International Human Resource Management: An Employment Relations Perspective*. London: Sage, pp. 37–56.

Alonso, L. E. (1999). *Trabajo y ciudadanía: estudios sobre la crisis de la sociedad salarial*. Madrid: Trotta.

Anderson, B. (2010). 'Migration, immigration controls and the fashioning of precarious workers', *Work, Employment and Society*, 24: 2, 300–317.

Anderson, B. and M. Ruhs (2010). 'Researching illegality and labour migration', *Population, Space and Place*, 16: 3, 175–179.

Appelbaum, E., R. Batt and I. Clark (2013). 'Implications of financial capitalism for employment relations research: evidence from breach of trust and implicit contracts in private equity buyouts', *Across Boundaries: The Global Challenges Facing Workers and Employment Research*, 51: 3, 498–518.

Aumayr-Pintar, C., S. Demetriades, D. Foden, V. Secpanovics and F. Wolf (2011). 'European company survey 2009', European Foundation for the Improvement of Living and Working Conditions. Available at: www.eurofound.europa.eu/publications/report/2010/working-conditions-industrial-relations/european-company-survey-2009-overview. [Accessed 1 May 2019].

Baccaro, L. and C. Howell (2017). *Trajectories of Neoliberal Transformation: European Industrial Relations since the 1970s*. Cambridge: Cambridge University Press.

Bachrach, P. and M. S. Baratz (1970). *Power and Poverty: Theory and Practice*. Oxford: Oxford University Press.

Baldamus, W. (1961). *Efficiency and Effort: An Analysis of Industrial Administration*. London: Tavistock Publications.

Bales, K., A. Bogg and T. Novitz (2018). '"Voice" and "choice" in modern working practices: problems with the Taylor Review', *Industrial Law Journal*, 47: 1, 46–75.

Bamber, G. J., J. H. Gittel, T. A. Kochan and A. Van Nordenflycht (2009). *Up in the Air: How Airlines Can Improve Performance by Engaging Employees*. New York: Cornell University Press.

Barlow, A. (2018). 'Shaping the future of parental leave', *The University of Manchester Magazine*. Available at: www.manchester.ac.uk/discover/magazine/features/shaping-the-future-of-parental-leave/. [Accessed 2 May 2017].

Barnard, C. (2012). *EU Employment Law*. Oxford: Oxford University Press.

Barrientos, S. (2001). 'Gender, flexibility and global value chains', *IDS Bulletin*, 32: 3, 83–93.

Barry, M. and A. Wilkinson (2016). 'Pro-social or pro-management? A critique of the conception of employee voice as a pro-social behaviour within organizational behaviour', *British Journal of Industrial Relations*, 54: 2, 261–284.

Batstone, E. (1988). 'The frontier of control', in D. Gallie (ed.) *Employment in Britain*. Oxford: Basil Blackwell, pp. 218–247.

Batt, R. (2018). 'The financial model of the firm, the "future of work", and employment relations', in A. Wilkinson, T. Dundon, J. Donaghey and A. Colvin (eds) *The Routledge Companion of Employment Relations*. London: Routledge, pp. 465–479.

Beaumont, P. B. and R. D. Harris (1992). 'Double-breasted recognition arrangements in Britain', *International Journal of Human Resources Management*, 3: 2, 267–283.

Behling, F. and M. Harvey (2015). 'The evolution of false self-employment in the British construction industry: a neo-Polanyian account of labour market formation', *Work, Employment and Society*, 29: 6, 969–988.

Bélanger, J. and P. Edwards (2007). 'The conditions promoting compromise in the workplace', *British Journal of Industrial Relations*, 45: 4, 713–734.

Bélanger, J. and P. Edwards (2013). 'The nature of front-line service work: distinctive features and continuity in the employment relationship', *Work, Employment and Society*, 27: 3, 433–450.

Benassi, C. (2013). 'Political economy of labour market segmentation: agency work in the automotive industry', ETUI Working Paper. Available at: www.etui.org/Publications2/Working-Papers/Political-economy-of-labour-market-segmentation-agency-work-in-the-automotive-industry. [Accessed 6 May 2019].

Berg, J. (2016). 'Income security in the on-demand economy: findings and policy lessons from a survey of crowdworkers', *Comparative Labor Law and Policy Journal*, 37: 3, 1–33.

Bergvall-Kåreborn, B. and D. Howcroft (2014). 'Amazon Mechanical Turk and the commodification of labour', *New Technology, Work and Employment*, 29: 3, 213–223.

Blackburn, D. and M. Puerto (2013). 'Colombia: the most dangerous place to be a trade unionist', in G. Gall and T. Dundon (eds) *Global Anti-Unionism: Nature, Dynamics, Trajectories and Outcomes*. London: Palgrave, pp. 184–206.

Blanpain, R. (ed.) (2014). *Comparative Labour Law and Industrial Relations in Industrialised Market Economies*. Netherlands: Kluwer Law International.

Bloodworth, J. (2018). 'I worked in an Amazon warehouse. Bernie Sanders is right to target them', *Guardian*. Available at: www.theguardian.com/commentisfree/2018/sep/17/amazon-warehouse-bernie-sanders. [Accessed 2 March 2019].

Bogg, A. (2012). 'Sham self-employment in the Supreme Court', *Industrial Law Journal*, 41: 3, 328–345.

Bolton, S. C. and K. Laaser (2013). 'Work, employment and society through the lens of moral economy', *Work, Employment and Society*, 27: 3, 508–525.

Brabham, D. (2012). 'The myth of amateur crowds: a critical discourse analysis of crowdsourcing coverage', *Information, Communication and Society*, 15: 3, 394–410.

Bridgman, T., S. Cummings and C. Mclaughlin (2016). 'Re-stating the case: how revisiting the development of the case method can help us think differently about the future of the business school', *Academy of Management Learning*, 15: 4, 724–741.

Buci-Glucksmann, C. (1980). *Gramsci and the State*. London: Lawrence & Wishart.

Budd, J. W. (2004). *Employment with a Human Face: Balancing Efficiency, Equity, and Voice*. London: Cornell University Press.

Budd, J. W. and S. Zagelmeyer (2010). 'Public policy and employee participation', in A. Wilkinson, P. J. Gollan, M. Marchington and D. Lewin (eds) *The Oxford Handbook of Participation in Organisations*. Oxford: Oxford University Press, pp. 476–503.

Burawoy, M. (2013). 'Ethnographic fallacies: reflections on labour studies in the era of market fundamentalism', *Work, Employment and Society*, 27: 3, 526–536.

Burnett, S. B., C. J. Gatrell, C. L. Cooper and P. Sparrow (2013). 'Fathers at work: a ghost in the organizational machine', *Gender, Work & Organization*, 20: 6, 632–646.

Butler, S. (2016). 'B&Q to raise basic wage: at the cost of pay for unsociable hours', *Guardian*. Available at: www.theguardian.com/society/2016/feb/05/bq-to-raise-basic-wage-at-the-cost-of-pay-for-unsociable-hours. [Accessed 3 March 2019].

Calo, R. and A. Rosenblat (2017). 'The talking economy: Uber, information and power', *Columbia Law Review*, 117, 1–68.

Cangiano, A. and K. Walsh (2014). 'Recruitment processes and immigration regulations: the disjointed pathways to employing migrant carers in ageing societies', *Work, Employment and Society*, 28: 3, 372–389.

Carney, G. M., T. Dundon and A. N. Leime (2012). 'Protecting the most vulnerable in an economic crisis: a participatory study of civil society organisations in Ireland', *Voluntary Sector Review*, 3: 3, 329–346.

Carter, R., A. Danford, D. Howcroft, H. Richardson, A. Smith and P. Taylor (2011). 'All they lack is a chain: lean and the new performance management in the British civil service', *New Technology, Work and Employment*, 26: 2, 83–97.

Castells, M. (1996). *The Rise of the Network Society: The Information Age*. Cambridge, MA: Blackwell Publishers.

Chamberlain, N. W. and J. W. Kuhn (1965). *Collective Bargaining*. New York: McGraw-Hill.

Chan, J., M. Selden and N. Pun (2020) *Dying for an iPhone: Apple, Foxconn, and the Lives of China's Workers*. Chicago: Haymarket Books; London: Pluto Press.

Cherry, M. A. (2016). 'Beyond misclassification: the digital transformation of work', *Comparative Labor Law and Policy Journal*, 27: 3, 596–597.

Child, J. (1997). 'Strategic choice in the analysis of action, structure, organizations and environment: retrospect and prospect', *Organization Studies*, 18: 1, 43–76.

CIPD (Chartered Institute of Personnel Development) (2013). 'Zero-hours contracts: myth and reality'. Available at: www.cipd.co.uk/Images/zero-hours-contracts_2013-myth-reality_tcm18–10710.pdf. [Accessed 20 March 2019].

CIPD (Chartered Institute of Personnel Development) (2015). 'Zero-hours and short-term contracts in the UK: employer and employee perspectives', CIPD Policy Report. London: Chartered Institute of Personnel and Development.

CIPD (Chartered Institute of Personnel Development) (2017). 'People management awards'. Available at: www.cipdpmas.co.uk/. [Accessed 20 January 2019].

Citizens UK (2017). Available at: www.citizensuk.org/. [Accessed 21 June 2017].

Clark, I. (2000). *Governance, the State, Regulation and Industrial Relations*. London: Routledge.

Clark, I. and T. Collings (2018). 'Work in Britain's informal economy: learning from road-side hand car washes', *British Journal of Industrial Relations*, 56 (2), 320–341.

Clark, J. (1985). 'The juridification of industrial relations: a review article', *Industrial Law Journal*, 14: 1, 69–90.

Clegg, H. A. (1972). 'Trade unions as an opposition which can never become a government', in W. E. McCarthy (ed.) *Trade Unions*. Harmondsworth: Penguin, pp. 74–86.

Collington, R. (2020). 'Denmark is helping those who can't work due to coronavirus: why isn't the UK?' Available at: www.theguardian.com/commentisfree/2020/mar/18/denmark-coronavirus-uk-government-workers-employees. [Accessed 11 May 2020].

Collins, H. (2001). 'Regulating the employment relation for competitiveness', *Industrial Law Journal*, 30: 1, 17–48.

Connolly, H., L. Krestsos and C. Phelan (2014a). *Radical Unions in Europe and the Future of Collective Interest Representation*. Bern: Peter Lang.

Connolly, H., S. Marino and M. Martínez Lucio (2014b). 'Trade union renewal and the challenges of representation: strategies towards migrant and ethnic minority workers in the Netherlands, Spain and the United Kingdom', *European Journal of Industrial Relations*, 20: 1, 5–20.

Connolly, H., S. Marino and M. Martínez Lucio (2019). *The Politics of Social Inclusion and Labor Representation: Immigrants and Trade Unions in the European Context*. Ithaca: Cornell University Press.

Countouris, N. (2018). 'Universality of rights', paper presented to Institute of Employment Rights conference on 'The Future of Labour Law: Progressive Rights under a Progressive Government', June 2018.

Craig, C., J. Rubery, R. Tarling and F. Wilkinson (1982). *Labour Market Structure, Industrial Organisation and Low Pay*. Cambridge: Cambridge University Press.

Cressey, P., J. Eldridge and J. MacInnes (1985). *Just Managing: Authority and Democracy in Industry*. Milton Keynes: Open University Press.

Cruz, K., K. Hardy and T. Saunders (2017). 'False self-employment, autonomy, and regulating for decent work: improving working conditions in the UK stripping industry', *British Journal of Industrial Relations*, 55: 1, 274–294.

Cullinane, N., E. Hickland, T. Dundon, T. Dobbins and J. Donaghey (2017). 'Triggering employee voice under the European Information and Consultation Directive: a non-union case study', *Economic and Industrial Democracy*, 37: 4, 629–655.

Cushen, J. and P. Thompson (2016). 'Financialization and value: why labour and the labour process still matter', *Work, Employment and Society*, 30: 2, 352–365.

Dahl, R. A. (1957). 'The concept of power', *Behavioral Science*, 2: 3, 201–215.

Danford, A., S. Durbin, M. Richardson, P. Stewart and S. Tailby (2013). 'Workplace partnership and professional workers: about as useful as a chocolate teapot?', *International Journal of Human Resource Management*, 25: 6, 879–894.

Darlington, R. (2002). 'Shop stewards' leadership, left-wing activism and collective workplace union organisation', *Capital and Class*, 26: 1, 95–126.

Darlington, R. and J. Dobson (2015). *The Conservative Government's Proposed Strike Ballot Thresholds: The Challenge to Trade Unions*. Liverpool: Institute of Employment Rights.

D'Art, D. and T. Turner (2002). 'The decline of worker solidarity and the end of collectivism?', *Economic and Industrial Democracy*, 23: 1, 7–34.

Datta, K., C. McIlwaine, Y. Evans, J. Herbert, J. May and J. Wills (2007). 'From coping strategies to tactics: London's low-pay economy and migrant labour', *British Journal of Industrial Relations*, 45: 2, 404–432.

Davis, J. (2017). 'Daddy's home: why on earth did I take shared parental leave?' *Guardian*. Available at: www.theguardian.com/lifeandstyle/2016/mar/27/shared-parental-leave-johnny-davis. [Accessed 20 November 2018].

Dawson, C., M. Veliziotis and B. Hopkins (2017). 'Understanding the perception of the "migrant work ethic"', *Work, Employment and Society*, 32: 5, 811–830.

DBEIS (Department for Business, Energy and Industrial Strategy) (2018a). 'Good work plan'. Available at: www.gov.uk/government/publications/good-work-plan. [Accessed 20 November 2018].

DBEIS (Department for Business, Energy and Industrial Strategy) (2018b). 'New "share the joy" campaign promotes shared parental leave rights for parents'. Available at: www.gov.uk/government/news/new-share-the-joy-campaign-promotes-shared-parental-leave-rights-for-parents. [Accessed 20 November 2018].

DBEIS (Department for Business, Energy and Industrial Strategy) (2019). *Protecting and Enhancing Worker Rights after the UK Withdrawal from the European Union*. London: DBEIS, CM66.

DBIS (Department of Business, Innovation and Skills) (2012). 'Employment law review: annual update'. Available at: www.gov.uk/government/publications/employment-law-review-2012. [Accessed 25 November 2018].

DBIS (Department of Business, Innovation and Skills) (2013). *Employment Law Review: Annual Update 2013*. London: DBIS.

Deakin, S. and G. S. Morris (2016). *Labour Law*. Oxford and Portland: Hart Publishing.

Deakin, S., S. Fraser Butlin, C. McLaughlin and A. Polanska (2015). 'Are litigation and collective bargaining complements or substitutes for achieving gender equality? A study of the British Equal Pay Act', *Cambridge Journal of Economics*, 39: 2, 381–403.

Degrauwe, J., G. Wisskirchen, G. Ormai, F. Spagnolo, F. Coutard, K. Van Kranenburg, K. Dulewicz, C. Gersbach, B. Hainz, C. Navarro, D. Yalçin, M. Lane, T. Matejovský and M. Novysedláková (2018). 'Employee representation and information, consultation and co-determination rights in Europe', *Thompson Reuters Practical Law*. Available at: https://uk.practicallaw.thomsonreuters.com/w-017–3200?transitionType=Default&contextData=(sc.Default)&firstPage=true&bhcp=1. [Accessed 28 June 2019].

Dehnen, V. and L. Pries (2014). 'International framework agreements: a thread in the web of transnational labour regulation', *European Journal of Industrial Relations*, 20: 4, 335–350.

De Stefano, V. (2016). 'The rise of the "just in time workforce": on demand work, crowd work and labour protection in the "gig economy"', International Labour Organisation. Available at: www.ecampus.itcilo. org/pluginfile.php/25267/mod_page/content/35/Conditions%20 of%20Work%20and%20Employment%20Series%20No.%2071.pdf. [Accessed 2 March 2019].

Dicken, P. (2007). *Global Shift*. London: Sage.

Dickens, L. (ed.) (2012). *Making Employment Rights Effective: Issues of Enforcement and Compliance*. Portland: Hart Publishing.

Dickens, L. and A. C. Neal (eds) (2006). *The Changing Institutional Face of British Employment Relations*. Alphen aan den Rijn: Kluwer Law International.

Dobbins, T. (2010). 'The case for beneficial constraints: why permissive voluntarism impedes workplace cooperation in Ireland', *Economic and Industrial Democracy*, 31: 4, 497–519.

Dobbins, T. and T. Dundon (2017). 'The chimera of sustainable labour-management partnership', *British Journal of Management*, 28: 3, 519–533.

Dobbins, T. and P. Gunnigle (2009). 'Can voluntary workplace partnership deliver sustainable mutual gains?', *British Journal of Industrial Relations*, 47: 3, 546–570.

Dobbins, T., T. Dundon, N. Cullinane, E. Hickland and J. Donaghey (2017). 'Employment regulation, game theory, and the lacuna in employee participation in liberal economies', *International Labour Review*, 156: 3/4, 395–422.

Doellgast, V., N. Lillie and V. Pulignano (2018). *Reconstructing Solidarity: Labour Unions, Precarious Work and the Politics of Institutional Change in Europe*. Oxford: Oxford University Press.

Donaghey, J. and J. Reinecke (2017). 'When industrial democracy meets corporate social responsibility: a comparison of the Bangladesh accord and alliance as responses to the Rana Plaza disaster', *British Journal of Industrial Relations*, 56: 1, 14–42.

Donaghey, J., N. Cullinane, T. Dundon and T. Dobbins (2012). 'Non-union representation, union avoidance and the managerial agenda: a case study', *Economic and Industrial Democracy*, 33: 2, 163–183.

Donovan (Lord) (chairperson) (1968). *Royal Commission on Trade Unions and Employers Associations Report*. Cmnd. 3623, London: HMSO.

Doussard, M. (2013). *Degraded Work: The Struggle at the Bottom of the Labor Market*. Minnesota: University of Minnesota Press.

DTI (Department for Trade and Industry) (1998). *Fairness at Work*. London: DTI, CM 3968.

Dundon, T. and T. Dobbins (2015). 'Militant partnership: a radical pluralist analysis of workforce dialectics', *Work, Employment and Society*,
29: 6, 1–20.

Dundon, T. and P. Gollan (2007). 'Re-conceptualising voice in the non-
union workplace', *International Journal of Human Resource Management*,
18: 7, 1182–1198.

Dundon, T. and A. Rafferty (2018). 'The (potential) demise of HRM?',
Human Resource Management Journal, 28: 3, 377–391.

Dundon, T. and D. Rollinson (2004). *Non-Union Employment Relations*.
London: Routledge.

Dundon, T. and D. Rollinson (2011). *Understanding Employment Relations*.
London: McGraw-Hill.

Dundon, T., M. A. González-Pérez and T. McDonough (2007). 'Bitten
by the Celtic Tiger: immigrant workers and industrial relations in the
new glocalized Ireland', *Economic and Industrial Democracy*, 28: 4,
501–522.

Dundon, T., N. Cullinane, J. Donaghey, T. Dobbins, A. Wilkinson and
E. Hickland (2014a). 'Double breasting employee voice: an assessment
of motives, arrangements and durability', *Human Relations*, 68: 3,
489–513.

Dundon, T., N. Cullinane, J. Donaghey, T. Dobbins, A. Wilkinson and
E. Hickland (2014b). 'Employer occupation of regulatory space of the
Employee Information and Consultation (I&C) Directive in liberal mar-
ket economies', *Work, Employment and Society*, 28: 1, 21–39.

Durbin, S., M. Page and S. Walby (2017). 'Gender equality and "austerity": vulnerabilities, resistance and change', *Gender, Work &
Organization*, 24: 1, 1–6.

Edwards, P. (1986). *Conflict at Work*. Oxford: Blackwell.

Edwards, P. K. (ed.) (1995). *Industrial Relations: Theory and Practice in
Britain*. Oxford: Blackwell.

Edwards, P. K. (2006). 'Power and ideology in the workplace: going
beyond even the second version of the three-dimensional view', *Work,
Employment and Society*, 20: 3, 571–581.

Edwards, P. K. (2014). 'Were the 40 years of "radical pluralism" a waste of
time?' *Warwick Papers in Industrial Relations*, 99: June.

Edwards, P., J. Bélanger and M. Wright (2006). 'The bases of compromise
in the workplace: a *theoretical* framework', *British Journal of Industrial
Relations*, 44: 1, 125–145.

Emmenegger, P., S. Hausermann, B. Palier and M. Seeleib-Kaiser
(2012). *The Age of Dualization: The Changing Face of Inequality in
Deindustrializing Societies*. Oxford: Oxford Scholarship Online.

Ewing, K. D. (1989). *Britain and the ILO*. Liverpool: Institute of Employment Rights.

Ewing, K. D., J. Hendy and C. Jones (eds) (2016). *A Manifesto for Labour Law: Towards a Comprehensive Revision of Workers' Rights*. Liverpool: Institute of Employment Rights.

Fagan, C., C. Lyonette, M. Smith and A. Saldaña-Tejeda (2012). *The Influence of Working Time Arrangements on Work-Life Integration or 'Balance': A Review of the International Evidence*. Geneva: ILO.

Fairris, D. and P. Askenazy (2010). 'Works councils and firm productivity in France', *Journal of Labor Research*, 31: 3, 209–229.

Fair Work Wales (2019). *Report of the Fair Work Commission*. Crown Copyright.

Featherstone, L. (2020). 'Unions are saving our lives everyday', *Jacobin*, 27 April. Available at: www.jacobinmag.com/2020/04/unions-coronavirus-covid-ppe-essential-workers-health-safety. [Accessed 12 May 2020].

Ferge, C. M. (2002). 'A critical assessment of the theoretical and empirical research on German works councils', *British Journal of Industrial Relations*, 40: 2, 221–248.

Findlay, P. and P. Thompson (2017). 'Contemporary work: its meanings and demands', *Journal of Industrial Relations*, 59: 2, 122–138.

Findlay, P., P. Thompson, C. Cooper and R. Pascoe-Deslauriers (2017). *The Value of Work: Who Benefits?* London: Chartered Institute of Personnel and Development. Available at: www.cipd.co.uk/Images/creating-and-capturing-value-at-work_2017-who-benefits-2_tcm18–33097.pdf. [Accessed 5 July 2019].

Fine, J. (2006). *Worker Centers: Organizing Communities at the Edge of the Dream*. New York: Cornell University Press.

Fine, J. and D. Tichenor (2009). 'A movement wrestling: American labor's enduring struggle with immigration, 1866–2007 – erratum/corrigendum', *Studies in American Political Development*, 23, 218–248.

Fine, J. and D. Tichenor (2012). 'An enduring dilemma: immigration organised labor in Western Europe and the United States', in M. R. Rosenblum and D. J. Tichenor, *The Oxford Handbook on the Politics of International Migration*. Oxford: Oxford University Press, pp. 532–572.

Fitzgerald, I. and J. Hardy (2010). 'Thinking outside of the box? Trade union organizing strategies and Polish migrant workers in the United Kingdom', *British Journal of Industrial Relations*, 48: 1, 131–150.

Fitzgerald, I., J. Hardy and M. Martínez Lucio (2012). 'The Internet, employment and Polish migrant workers: communication, activism and competition in the new organisational spaces', *New Technology, Work and Employment*, 27: 2, 93–105.

Flanders, A. (1970). *Management and Unions*. London: Faber & Faber.

Flanders, A. (1974). 'The tradition of voluntarism', *British Journal of Industrial Relations*, 12: 3, 352–370.

Fleming, P. and A. Spicer (2014). 'Power in management and organization science', *Academy of Management Journal*, 8: 1, 237–298.

Ford, M. (2013). 'Employer anti-unionism in democratic Indonesia', in G. Gall and T. Dundon (eds), *Global Anti-Unionism: Nature, Dynamics, Trajectories and Outcomes*. London: Palgrave, pp. 224–243.

Ford, M. (2015). *The Rise of the Robots*. New York: Basic Books.

Ford, M. (2016). 'Workers' rights from Europe: the impact of Brexit', Trade Union Congress. Available at: www.tuc.org.uk/sites/default/files/Brexit%20Legal%20Opinion.pdf. [Accessed 2 March 2019].

Ford, M. and T. Novitz (2016). 'Legislating for control: the Trade Union Act 2016', *Industrial Law Journal*, 45: 3, 277–298.

Forde, C. and R. MacKenzie (2010). 'The ethical agendas of employment agencies towards migrant workers in the UK: deciphering the codes', *Journal of Business Ethics*, 97: 1, 31–41.

Fox, A. (1966). 'Industrial sociology and industrial relations', Royal Commission on Trade Unions and Employer Association. London: Her Majesty's Stationery Office.

Fox, A. (1974). *Beyond Contract: Work, Power and Trust Relations*. London: Faber & Faber.

Frame, J. (2017). 'Exploring the approaches to care of faith-based and secular NGOs in Cambodia that serve victims of trafficking, exploitation, and those involved in sex work', *International Journal of Sociology and Social Policy*, 37: 5/6, 311–326.

Freedland, M. (2003). *The Personal Employment Contract*. Oxford: Oxford University Press.

French, J. R. and B. Raven (1959). 'The bases of social power', in J. Shafritz, J. S. Ott and Y. Suk Jag (eds) *Classics of Organization Theory*. Boston: Cengage Learning, pp. 251–260.

Frey, C. and A. Osborne (2017). 'The future of employment: how susceptible are jobs to computerisation?', *Technological Forecasting and Social Change*, 114: 1, 254–280.

Friedman, T. (2005). *The World is Flat*. New York: Allen Lane.

Gall, G. and T. Dundon (eds) (2013). *Global Anti-Unionism: Nature, Dynamics, Trajectories and Outcomes*. Basingstoke: Palgrave Macmillan.

Garrahan, P. and P. Stewart (1992). *The Nissan Enigma: Flexibility at Work in a Local Economy*. London: Mansell.

Geelan, T. and A. Hodder (2017). 'Enhancing transnational labour solidarity: the unfulfilled promise of the Internet and social media', *Industrial Relations Journal*, 48: 4, 345–364.

Gillespie, T. (2014). 'The relevance of algorithms', in T. Gillespie, P. Boczhowski and K. Foot (eds) *Media Technologies*. Cambridge, MA: MIT Press, pp. 167–193.

Gold, M. and I. Artus (2015). 'Employee participation in Germany', in S. Johnstone and P. Ackers (eds) *Finding a Voice at Work? New Perspectives on Employment Relations*. Oxford: Oxford University Press, pp. 193–217.

Gold, M. and J. Waddington (2019). 'Introduction: board-level employee representation in Europe: state of play', *European Journal of Industrial Relations*, 25: 3, 205–218.

Gollan, P. J. and R. Markey (2001). 'Conclusions: models of diversity and interaction', in R. Markey, P. J. Gollan, A. Hodgkinson, A. Chouraqui and U. Veersma (eds) *Models of Employee Participation in a Changing Global Environment: Diversity and Interaction*. Aldershot: Ashgate, pp. 322–343.

Goodrich, C. (1921). *The Frontier of Control*. London: Harcourt, Brace and Company.

Grady, J. and M. Simms (2018). 'Trade unions and the challenge of fostering solidarities in an era of financialisation', *Economic and Industrial Democracy*, 40: 3, 490–510.

Green, F. and S. McIntosh (2007). 'Is there a genuine underutilisation of skills amongst the over-qualified?', *Applied Economics*, 39: 4, 427–439.

Greene, A. M., J. Hogan and M. Grieco (2003). 'Commentary: e-collectivism and distributed discourse: new opportunities for trade union democracy', *Industrial Relations Journal*, 34: 4, 282–289.

Greer, I. and M. Hauptmeier (2016). 'Management whipsawing: the staging of labor competition under globalization', *International Labor Review*, 69: 1, 29–52.

Grimshaw, D. and M. Carroll (2006). 'Adjusting to the national minimum wage: constraints and incentives to change in six low-paying sectors', *Industrial Relations Journal*, 37: 1, 22–47.

Grimshaw, D. and S. Hayter (2020). 'Employment relations and economic performance', in C. Frege and J. Kelly (eds) *Comparative Employment Relations in the Global Economy*, 2nd edition. London: Routledge, pp. 139–167.

Grimshaw, D., M. Johnson, J. Rubery and A. Keizer (2016). 'Reducing precarious work in Europe through social dialogue: protective gaps and the role of social dialogue in Europe', Report for the European Commission,

Institute of Work, Skills and Training. Available at: www.research.mbs. ac.uk/ewerc/Portals/0/.../comparative-research-briefing-english.pdf. [Accessed 15 May 2019].

Hall, M. (2010). 'EU regulation and the UK employee consultation framework', *Economic and Industrial Democracy*, 31: 4, 55–69.

Hall, M. and J. Purcell (2012). *Consultation at Work: Regulation and Practice*. Oxford: Oxford University Press.

Hall, M., S. Hutchinson, J. Purcell, M. Terry and J. Parker (2011). 'Promoting effective consultation? Assessing the impact of the ICE Regulations', *British Journal of Industrial Relations*, 51: 2, 355–381.

Hall, P. A. and D. Soskice (eds) (2001). *Varieties of Capitalism: The Institutional Foundations of Comparative Advantage*. Oxford: Oxford University Press, pp. 71–103.

Hancher, L. and M. Moran (1989). 'Organizing regulatory space', in L. Hancher and M. Moran (eds) *Capitalism, Culture and Economic Regulation*. Oxford: Clarendon Press, pp. 271–299.

Harvey, D. (2006). *Spaces of Global Capitalism: A Theory of Uneven Geographical Development*. London: Verso.

Healy, G. and G. Kirton (2000). 'Women, power and trade union government in the UK', *British Journal of Industrial Relations*, 38: 3, 343–360.

Hebson, G. and J. Rubery (2018). 'Employment relations and gender equality', in A. Wilkinson, T. Dundon, J. Donaghey and A. Colvin (eds) *The Routledge Companion to Employment Relations*. London: Routledge, pp. 93–107.

Heery, E. (2009). 'Trade unions and contingent labour: scale and method', *Cambridge Journal of Regions, Economy and Society*, 2: 3, 429–442.

Heery, E. (2016). *Framing Work*. Oxford: Oxford University Press.

Heery, E. and C. Frege (2006). 'New actors in industrial relations', *British Journal of Industrial Relations*, 44: 4, 601–604.

Heery, E., B. Abbott and S. Williams (2012a). 'The involvement of civil society organizations in British industrial relations: extent, origins and significance', *British Journal of Industrial Relations*, 50: 1, 47–72.

Heery, E., D. Hann and D. Nash (2017). 'The Living Wage campaign in the UK', *Employee Relations*, 39: 6, 800–814.

Heery, E., S. Williams and B. Abbott (2012b). 'Civil society organizations and trade unions: cooperation, conflict, indifference', *Work, Employment and Society*, 26: 1, 145–160.

Hendry, K. and K. Ewing (2017). *The Purposes and Benefits of Sectoral Collective Bargaining*. Liverpool: Institute of Employment Rights.

Hepple, B. (2005). *Labour Laws and Global Trade*. Oxford: Hart Publishing.

Higgins, M. D. (2019). *Changing Work in a Crisis-Stricken World: The Need to Embrace a New Paradigm*. Lecture delivered to ILO Centenary Conference, Dublin Castle, 17 September 2019.

Hirst, P. and G. Thompson (1999). *Globalisation in Question*. Cambridge: Polity Press.

Hoch, M. (2006). *Roads to Post-Fordism: Labour Markets and Social Structures in Europe*. Ashgate: Aldershot.

Hodder, A. (2014). 'Organising young workers in the Public and Commercial Services Union', *Industrial Relations Journal*, 45: 2, 153–168.

Hodder, A. and D. Houghton (2015). 'Union use of social media: a study of the University and College Union on Twitter', *New Technology Work and Employment*, 30: 3, 173–189.

Holgate, J. (2015). 'Community organising in the UK: a "new" approach for trade unions?', *Economic and Industrial Democracy*, 36: 3, 431–455.

Holgate, J., J. Keles, A. Pollert and L. Kumarappen (2012). 'Workplace problems among Kurdish workers in London: experiences of an "invisible" community and the role of community organisations as support networks', *Journal of Ethnic and Migration Studies*, 38: 4, 595–612.

Holmes, C. and K. Mayhew (2012). *The Changing Shape of the UK Job Market and its Implications for the Bottom Half of Earners*. London: Resolution Foundation.

Howcroft, D. and B. Bergvall-Kåreborn (2019). 'A typology of crowdwork platforms', *Work, Employment and Society*, 33: 1, 21–38.

Howcroft, D. and P. Taylor (2014). ' "Plus ca change, plus la meme chose?": researching and theorising the "new" new technologies', *New Technology, Work and Employment*, 29: 1, 1–8.

Howell, C. (2005). *Trade Unions and the State: The Construction of Industrial Relations Institutions in Britain, 1890–2000*. Princeton: Princeton University Press.

Hyman, R. (1975). *Industrial Relations: A Marxist Introduction*. London: Palgrave.

Hyman, R. (2005). 'Shifting dynamics in international trade unionism: agitation, organisation, bureaucracy, diplomacy', *Labor History*, 46: 2, 137–154.

Hyman, R. (2008). 'The state in industrial relations', in P. Blyton, N. Bacon, J. Fiorito and E. Heery (eds) *The Sage Handbook in Industrial Relations*. London: Sage Publications, pp. 248–283.

Hyman, R. (2015a). 'The very idea of democracy at work', *Transfer: European Review of Labour and Research*, 22: 1, 11–24.

Hyman, R. (2015b). 'Three scenarios for industrial relations in Europe', *International Labour Review*, 154: 1, 5–14.

ILO (International Labour Organization) and OECD (Organisation for Economic Co-operation and Development) (2015). 'The labour share in G20 economies, report prepared for the G20 Employment Working Group, Antalya, Turkey', OECD. Available at: www.oecd.org/g20/topics/employment-and-social-policy/The-Labour-Share-in-G20-Economies.pdf. [Accessed 1 June 2019].

IMF (International Monetary Fund) (2017a). 'World economic outlook: seeking sustainable growth: short-term recovery, long-term challenges'. Available at: www.imf.org/en/Publications/WEO/Issues/2017/09/19/world-economic-outlook-october-2017. [Accessed 1 February 2019].

IMF (International Monetary Fund) (2017b). 'World economic outlook: gaining momentum?'. Available at: www.imf.org/en/Publications/WEO/Issues/2017/04/04/world-economic-outlook-april-2017. [Accessed 1 February 2019].

Ince, A., D. Featherstone, A. Cumbers, D. MacKinnon and K. Strauss (2015). 'British jobs for British workers? Negotiating work, nation, and globalisation through the Lindsey Oil Refinery disputes', *Antipode*, 47: 1, 139–157.

Jacoby, S. (2005). *The Embedded Corporation: Corporate Governance and Employment Relations in Japan and the United States*. Princeton: Princeton University Press.

Johnson, M. (2017). 'Implementing the living wage in UK local government', *Employee Relations*, 39: 6, 840–849.

Johnston, J. and C. Land-Kazlauskas (2017). 'On demand and organized: developing collective agency, representation and bargaining in the gig economy', 5th Conference of the Regulating for Decent Work Network. Geneva: ILO.

Johnstone, S. and P. Ackers (eds) (2015). *Finding a Voice at Work? New Perspectives on Employment Relations*. Oxford: Oxford University Press.

Johnstone, S. and A. Wilkinson (2018). 'The potential of labour–management partnership: a longitudinal case analysis', *British Journal of Management*, 29: 3, 554–570.

Joint Committee on Human Rights (2018). 'Enforcing human rights', *House of Commons Paper* 669, *House of Lords Paper* 171, published 19 July 2018.

Jordan, E., A. P. Thomas, J. W. Kitching and R. A. Blackburn (2013). 'Employment regulation part A: employer perceptions and the impact of employment regulation', DBIS Employment Relations Research Series, 123. Available at: https://assets.publishing.service.gov.uk/government/uploads/system/uploads/attachment_data/file/128792/13–638-employer-perceptions-and-the-impact-of-employment-regulation.pdf. [Accessed 30 November 2018].

Kahn-Freund, O. (1977). *Labour and the Law*. London: Stevens and Sons.

Kaine, S. (2020). 'Union voice', in A. Wilkinson, J. Donaghey, T. Dundon and R. Freeman (eds) *Handbook of Research on Employee Voice*. Cheltenham: Edward Elgar Publishing, pp. 170–187.

Kalleberg, A. (2000). 'Nonstandard employment relations: part-time, temporary and contract work', *Annual Review of Sociology*, 26: 1, 341–365.

Kalleberg, A. (2011). *Good Jobs, Bad Jobs: The Rise of Polarized and Precarious Employment Systems in the United States, 1970s to 2000s*. New York: Russell Sage Foundation.

Karamessini, M. and J. Rubery (eds) (2013). *Women and Austerity: The Economic Crisis and the Future for Gender Equality*. Oxford: Routledge.

Karanikolos, M., P. Mladovsky, J. Cylus, S. Thomson, S. Basu, D. Stuckler, J. P. Mackenbach, and M. McKee (2013). 'Financial crisis, austerity, and health in Europe', *The Lancet*, 381: 9874, 1323–1331.

Kaufman, B. E. (2008). *Managing the Human Factor: The Early Years of Human Resource Management in American Industry*. Ithaca: Cornell University Press.

Kaufman, B. E. and M. Barry (2014). 'IR theory built on the founders' principles with empirical application to Australia', *ILR Review*, 67: 4, 1203–1234.

Kaufman, B. E. and G. Gall (2015). 'Advancing industrial relations theory: an analytical synthesis of British-American and pluralist-radical ideas', *Relations Industrielles/Industrial Relations*, 70: 3, 407–431.

Kaufman, B. E. and D. G. Taras (eds) (2000). *Non-Union Employee Representation: History, Contemporary Practice and Policy*. New York: M.E. Sharpe.

Kautonen, T., S. Down, F. Welter, P. Vainio, K. Althoff and S. Kolb (2010). ' "Involuntary self-employment" as a public policy issue: a cross-country European review', *International Journal of Entrepreneurial Behaviour & Research*, 16: 2, 112–129.

Kelly, J. (1998). *Rethinking Industrial Relations: Mobilisation, Collectivism and Long Waves*. London: Routledge.

Kelly, J. (2011). 'Theories of collective action and union power', in G. Gall, A. Wilkinson and R. Hurd (eds) *International Handbook on Labour Unions: Responses to Neo-Liberalism*. Cheltenham: Edward Elgar, pp. 13–29.

Keune, M. and A. Serrano (eds) (2014). *Deconstructing Flexicurity and Developing Alternative Approaches: Towards New Concepts and Approaches for Employment and Social Policy*. Abingdon: Routledge.

Kirk, E. (2018). 'The (re)organisation of conflict at work: mobilisation, counter-mobilisation and the displacement of grievance expressions', *Economic and Industrial Democracy*, 39: 4, 639–660.

Kirton, G. (2006). 'Alternative and parallel career paths for women: the case of trade union participation', *Work, Employment and Society*, 20: 1, 47–65.

Kirton, G. (2015). 'Progress towards gender democracy in UK unions 1987–2012', *British Journal of Industrial Relations*, 53: 3, 484–507.

Kirton, G. and G. Healy (1999). 'Transforming union women: the role of women trade union officials in union renewal', *Industrial Relations Journal*, 30: 1, 31–45.

Kirton, G. and G. Healy (2012). ' "Lift as you rise": union women's leadership talk', *Human Relations*, 65: 8, 979–999.

Kirton, G. and G. Healy (2013). 'Commitment and collective identity of long-term union participation: the case of women union leaders in the UK and USA', *Work Employment and Society*, 27: 2, 195–212.

Kirton, H. (2017). 'Taylor Review will "further complicate" employment law', CIPD. Available at: www2.cipd.co.uk/pm/peoplemanagement. [Accessed 2 April 2019].

Kochan, T. and P. Osterman (1994). *The Mutual Gains Enterprise: Forging a Winning Partnership among Labour, Management and Government*. Boston: Harvard Business School Press.

Kochan, T., H. C. Katz and R. B. McKersie (1986). *The Transformation of American Industrial Relations*. Ithaca: Cornell University Press.

Kochan, T., W. T. Kimball, D. Yang and E. L. Kelly (2019). 'Worker voice in America: is there a gap between what workers expect and what they experience?', *Industrial and Labor Relations Review*, 72: 1, 3–38.

Kochan, T., P. Adler, R. McKersie, A. Eaton, P. Segal and P. Gerhart (2008). 'The potential and precariousness of partnership: the case of the Kaiser Permanente Labour Management Partnership', *Industrial Relations*, 47: 1, 36–66.

Koukiadaki, A., I. Távora and M. Martínez Lucio (eds) (2016). *Joint Regulation and Labour Market Policy in Europe during the Crisis*. Brussels: European Trade Union Institute.

Laaser, K. (2010). ' "If you are having a go at me, I am going to have a go at you": the changing nature of social relationships of bank work under performance management', *Work, Employment and Society*, 30: 6, 1000–1016.

Lansley, S. (2011). *Britain's Livelihood Crisis*. London: TUC.

Lash, S. and J. Urry (1987). *The End of Organized Capitalism*. Cambridge: Polity Press.

Lavelle, J., P. Gunnigle and A. McDonnell (2010). 'Patterning employee voice in multinational companies', *Human Relations*, 63: 1, 395–418.

Lazonick, W. and M. O'Sullivan (2000). 'Maximising shareholder value: a new ideology for corporate governance', *Economy and Society*, 29: 1, 13–35.

Lee, E. H. (1997). *Labour Movement and the Internet: The New Internationalism.* London: Pluto Press.

Lee, M. K., D. Kusbit, E. Metsky and L. Dabbish (2015). 'Working with machines: the impact of algorithmic and data-driven management on human workers', 33rd Annual ACM Conference on Human Factors in Computing, Seoul, April 2015.

Legal Action Group (2016). *Justice in Free Fall: A Report on the Decline of Civil Legal Aid in England and Wales.* Available at: www.lag.org.uk. [Accessed 6 July 2017].

Lehdonvitra, V. (2016). 'Algorithms that divide and unite: delocalisation, identity and collective action in microwork', in J. Flecker (ed.) *Space, Place and Global Digital Work.* London: Palgrave Macmillan, pp. 53–80.

Lenaerts, K., Z. Kilhoffer and M. Akgüç (2018). 'Traditional and new forms of organisation and representation in the platform economy', *Work Organisation, Labour and Globalisation*, 12: 2, 60–78.

Lewis, R. (1976). 'The historical development of labour law', *British Journal of Industrial Relations*, 14: 1, 1–17.

Lillie, N. and M. Martínez Lucio (2012). 'Rollerball and the spirit of capitalism: competitive dynamics within the global context, the challenge to labour transnationalism, and the emergence of ironic outcomes', *Critical Perspectives on International Business*, 8: 1, 74–92.

Lipietz, A. (1997). 'The post-Fordist world: labour relations, international hierarchy and global ecology', *Review of International Political Economy*, 4: 1, 1–41.

Lipsky, D. B. and H. S. Farber (1976). 'The composition of strike activity in the construction industry', *Industrial and Labor Relations Review*, 29: 3, 388–204.

Littler, C. (1993). 'Industrial relations theory: a political economy perspective', in R. J. Adams and N. M. Meltz (eds) *Industrial Relations Theory: Its Nature, Scope and Pedagogy.* New Jersey: Scarecrow Press, pp. 1–16.

Liversage, A. (2009). 'Vital conjunctures, shifting horizons: high-skilled female immigrants looking for work', *Work, Employment and Society*, 23: 1, 120–141.

Logan, J. (2013). 'Employer opposition in the United States: anti-union campaigning from the 1950s to the present', in G. Gall and T. Dundon (eds) *Global Anti-Unionism.* London: Palgrave, pp. 21–28.

Loosie, J. K., N. Torka and J. E. Wigboldus (2010). 'Participation and organizational performance', in F. Garibaldo and V. Telljohann (eds) *The Ambivalent Character of Participation.* Frankfurt: Peter Lang, pp. 327–339.

Lukes, S. (1974). *Power: A Radical View*. London: Macmillan.

Lukes, S. (2005). *Power: A Radical View*, 2nd edition. Basingstoke: Macmillan.

Lydersen, C. (2018). 'I'm not on the menu: McDonald's workers strike over "rampant" sexual harassment', *Guardian*. Available at: www.the-guardian.com/business/2018/sep/18/mcdonalds-workers-strike-over-rampant-sexual-harassment. [Accessed 20 November 2018].

McAfee, A. and E. Brynjolfsson (2014). *The Second Machine Age*. New York: W. W. Norton and Co.

McAfee, A. and E. Brynjolfsson (2017). *Machine, Platform, Crowd: Harnessing the Digital Revolution*. London: W. W. Norton.

McBride, A. (2002). *Gender Democracy in Trade Unions*. London: Routledge.

McBride, J. and I. Greenwood (2009). *Community Unionism*. New York: Palgrave Macmillan.

McBride, J. and M. Martínez Lucio (2011). 'Dimensions of collectivism: occupation, community and the increasing role of memory and personal dynamics in the debate', *Work, Employment and Society*, 25: 4, 794–805.

McBride, J. and M. Martínez Lucio (2016). 'Disaggregating and aggregating work: workers, management and the struggle over creating coherency and purpose in a context of work degradation', *Human Resource Management Journal*, 26: 4, 490–504.

McCollum, D. and A. Findlay (2015). '"Flexible" workers for "flexible" jobs? The labour market function of A8 migrant labour in the UK', *Work, Employment and Society*, 29: 3, 427–443.

McDonough, T. and T. Dundon (2010). 'Thatcherism delayed? The Irish crisis and the paradox of social partnership', *Industrial Relations Journal*, 41: 6, 544–562.

Machin, S. and R. Costa (2017). 'What's happening with real wages and living standards in the UK?', *LSE Business Review*. Available at: www.blogs.lse.ac.uk/businessreview/2017/06/01/whats-happening-with-real-wages-and-living-standards-in-the-uk/. [Accessed 20 November 2018].

McIlroy, J. (1991). *The Permanent Revolution? Conservative Law and the Trade Unions*. London: Spokesman Books.

McIlroy, J. (2011). 'Britain: how neo-liberalism cut unions down to size', in G. Gall, A. Wilkinson and R. Hurd (eds) *The International Handbook of Labour Unions: Responses to Neo-Liberalism*. Cheltenham: Edward Elgar, pp. 82–103.

McKay, S., S. Jefferys, A. Paraksevopoulou and J. Kels (2012). 'Study on precarious work and social rights. European Commission', Working

Lives Research Institute. Available at: https://ec.europa.eu/social/ BlobServlet?docId=7925&langId=en. [Accessed 1 July 2019].

MacKenzie, R. and M. Martínez Lucio (2005). 'The realities of regulatory change: beyond the fetish of deregulation', *Sociology*, 39: 3, 499–517.

MacKenzie, R. and M. Martínez Lucio (2014). 'Regulating work and employment internationally: the emergence of soft regulation', in M. Martínez Lucio (ed.) *International HRM: An Employment Relations Perspective*. London: SAGE Publications, pp. 238–254.

McNulty, Y., R. McPhail, C. Inversi, T. Dundon and E. Nachanska (2018). 'Employee voice mechanisms for lesbian, gay, bisexual and transgender expatriation: the role of Employee-Resource Groups (ERGs) and allies', *International Journal of Human Resource Management*, 29: 5, 829–856.

Marchington, M. (2015). 'Analysing the forces shaping employee involvement and participation (EIP) at organisation level in liberal market economies (LMEs)', *Human Resource Management Journal*, 25: 1, 1–18.

Marchington, M., D. Grimshaw, J. Rubery and H. Willmott (eds) (2005). *Fragmenting Work Blurring Organizational Boundaries and Disordering Hierarchies*. Oxford: Oxford University Press.

Marino, S., R. Penninx and J. Rossblad (eds) (2017). *Trade Unions, Immigration and Immigrants in Europe in the 21st Century: New Approaches under Changed Conditions*. Geneva: ILO; Cheltenham: Edward Elgar.

Marks, G. W. (2014). *Unions in Politics: Britain, Germany, and the United States in the Nineteenth and Early Twentieth Centuries*. New Jersey: Princeton University Press.

Martínez Lucio, M. (2006). 'Trade unionism and the realities of change', in L. E. Alonso and M. Martínez Lucio (eds) *Employment Relations in a Changing Society*. Basingstoke: Palgrave Macmillan, pp. 200–214.

Martínez Lucio, M. (2016a). *Capital and Labour: The Shifting Terrains of Struggle and Accommodation in Labour and Employment Relations*. London: Sage Publications.

Martínez Lucio, M. (2016b). 'Myths and fantasies in discussing the end of organised labour: what do we mean when we say there is a crisis of labour relations?', in P. Elgoibar, M. Euwema and L. Manduate (eds), *Building Trust and Constructive Conflict Management in Organization*. Switzerland: Springer International, pp. 15–28.

Martínez Lucio, M. (2018). 'The return of the political or the re-thinking of the political? Appreciating the nature of recent developments in the industrial relations discipline', BUIRA Annual Conference, Middlesex University, July 2018.

Martínez Lucio, M. and H. Connolly (2012). 'Transformation and continuities in urban struggles: urban politics, trade unions and migration in Spain', *Urban Studies*, 49: 3, 669–684.

Martínez Lucio, M. and R. MacKenzie (2017). 'The state and the regulation of work and employment: theoretical contributions, forgotten lessons and new forms of engagement', *The International Journal of Human Resource Management*, 28: 21, 2983–3002.

Martínez Lucio, M. and R. MacKenzie (2018). 'The state and employment relations: continuity and change in the politics of regulation', in A. Wilkinson, T. Dundon, J. Donaghey and A. Colvin (eds) *The Routledge Companion to Employment Relations*. Oxford: Oxford University Press, pp. 157–174.

Martínez Lucio, M. and R. Perrett (2009). 'The diversity and politics of trade unions' responses to minority ethnic and migrant workers: the context of the UK', *Economic and Industrial Democracy*, 30: 3, 324–347.

Martínez Lucio, M. and M. Stuart (2004). 'Swimming against the tide: social partnership, mutual gains and the revival of "tired" HRM', *International Journal of Human Resource Management*, 15: 2, 410–424.

Martínez Lucio, M. and M. Stuart (2005). 'Partnership and new industrial relations in a risk society: an age of shotgun weddings and marriages of convenience?', *Work, Employment and Society*, 19: 4, 797–817.

Martínez Lucio, M. and M. Stuart (2011). 'The state, public policy and the renewal of HRM', *International Journal of Human Resource Management*, 22: 18, 3661–3671.

Martínez Lucio, M., S. Marino and H. Connolly (2017). 'Organising as a strategy to reach precarious and marginalised workers: a review of debates on the role of the political dimension and the dilemmas of representation and solidarity', *Transfer: European Review of Labour and Research*, 23: 1, 31–46.

Martínez Lucio, M., S. Walker and P. Trevorrow (2009). 'Making networks and (re)making trade union bureaucracy: a European-wide case study of trade union engagement with the Internet and networking', *New Technology, Work and Employment*, 24: 2, 115–130.

Marx, K. (1932). *Capital, the Communist Manifesto and Other Writings*. New York: Modern Library.

Mason, P. (2016). *Post-Capitalism: A Guide to Our Future*. London: Allen Lane.

Mazzucato, M. (2015). *The Entrepreneurial State: Debunking Public vs. Private Sector Myths*. London: Anthem Press.

Mazzucato, M. (2019). *The Value of Everything: Making and Talking in the Global Economy*. London: Penguin Books.

Meardi, G., M. Simms and D. Adam (2019). 'Trade unions and precariat in Europe: representative claims', *European Journal of
Industrial Relations*, On-Line Early. https://doi.org/10.1177/
0959680119863585.

Metcalf, D. (2018). 'United Kingdom labour market enforcement strategy 2018/19', DBEIS. Available at: www.gov.uk/government/publica-
tions/labour-market-enforcement-strategy-2018-to-2019. [Accessed 20
March 2019].

Morrison, E. (2011). 'Employee voice behaviour: integration and direc-
tions for future research', *Academy of Management Annals*, 5: 1, 373–412.

Mustchin, S. and M. Martínez Lucio (2017). 'Transnational collective
agreements and the development of new spaces for union action: the formal and informal uses of international and European framework agreements in the UK', *British Journal of Industrial Relations*, 55: 3, 577–601.

Mustchin, S. and M. Martínez Lucio (2020). 'The evolving nature of
labour inspection, enforcement of employment rights and the regulatory
reach of the state in Britain', *Journal of Industrial Relations*, On-Line
First. https://doi.org/10.1177/0022185620908909.

Ness, I. (2016). *Southern Insurgency: The Coming of the Global Working
Class*. London: Pluto Press.

Nienhüser, W. (2020). 'Works councils', in A. Wilkinson, J. Donaghey, T.
Dundon and R. B. Freeman (eds) *Handbook of Research on Employee
Voice*. Cheltenham: Edward Elgar, pp. 247–263.

Nolan, P. and P. Marginson (1990). 'Skating on thin ice? David Metcalf
on trade unions and productivity', *British Journal of Industrial Relations*,
28: 2, 227–247.

Novak, P. (2020). 'Putting people's health before profit', *The Chartist*,
30 March. Available at: www.chartist.org.uk/putting-peoples-health-
before-profit/. [Accessed 2 April 2020].

OECD (Organization for Economic Co-operation and Development)
(2014). 'The OECD indicators on Employment Protection Legislation'.
Available at: www.oecd.org/employment/emp/oecdindicatorsofem-
ploymentprotection.htm. [Accessed 13 May 2020].

OECD (Organization for Economic Co-operation and Development)
(2017). 'Trade union density figure by country'. Available at: www.oecd-
ilibrary.org/economics/economic-policy-reforms-2017/coverage-rates-
of-collective-bargaining-agreements-and-trade-union-density-rates_
growth-2017-graph183-en. [Accessed 20 March 2019].

ONS (Office for National Statistics) (2016). 'Trends in self-employment in
the UK: 2001 to 2015'. Available at: www.ons.gov.uk/employmentand-
labourmarket/peopleinwork/employmentandemployeetypes/articles/
trendsinselfemploymentintheuk/2001to2015. [Accessed 1 August 2017].

ONS (Office for National Statistics) (2019). 'Trade union membership 2018'. Available at: www.assets.publishing.service.gov.uk/government/uploads/system/uploads/attachment_data/file/805268/trade-union-membership-2018-statistical-bulletin.pdf. [Accessed 1 April 2019].

O'Sullivan, M., T. Turner, J. McMahon, L. Ryan, J. Lavelle, C. Murphy, M. O'Brien and P. Gunnigle (2015). *A Study on the Prevalence of Zero Hours Contracts among Irish Employers and their Impact on Employees*. University of Limerick. Available at: www.labour.ie/download/pdf/studyontheprevalenceofzerohourscontracts.pdf.

Parker, M. (2015). 'Between sociology and the B-school: critical studies of organisation, work and employment in the UK', *Sociological Review*, 63: 1, 162–180.

Parliament UK (2018). 'Fathers and the workplace', Parliamentary Publications. Available at: www.publications.parliament.uk/pa/cm201719/cmselect/cmwomeq/358/35802.htm. [Accessed 28 November 2019].

Paugam, S. (2005). *Les Formes élémentaires de la pauvreté*. Paris: PUF.

PCAW (2017). *Public Concern at Work*. Available at: www.pcaw.org.uk/. [Accessed 10 July 2017]

Peck, F., G. Mulvey, K. Jackson and J. Jackson (2012), 'Business perceptions of regulatory burden', DBEIS. Available at: www.bis.gov.uk/assets/biscore/better-regulation/docs/b/12–913-business-perceptions-of-regulatory-burden.pdf. [Accessed 20 March 2019].

Però, D. (2019). 'Indie unions, organizing and labour renewal: learning from precarious migrant workers', *Work, Employment and Society*, On-Line First. https://doi.org/10.1177/0950017019885075.

Perrett, R. (2007). 'Worker voice in the context of the re-regulation of employment: employer tactics and statutory union recognition in the UK', *Work, Employment and Society*, 21: 4, 617–634.

Perrett, R. and M. Martínez Lucio (2008). 'The challenge of connecting and co-ordinating the learning agenda: a case study of a trade union learning centre in the UK', *Employee Relations*, 30: 6, 623–639.

Perrett, R. and M. Martínez Lucio (2009). 'Trade unions and relations with black and minority-ethnic community groups in the United Kingdom: the development of new alliances?', *Journal of Ethnic and Migration Studies*, 35: 8, 1295–1314.

Perrett, R., M. Martínez Lucio, J. McBride and S. Craig (2012). 'Trade union learning strategies and migrant workers: policies and practice in a new-liberal environment', *Urban Studies*, 49: 3, 649–667.

Pfau-Effinger, B. (1998). 'Culture or structure as explanations for differences in part-time work in Germany, Finland and the Netherlands?', in J. O'Reilly and C. Fagan (eds) *Part-Time Prospects; Part-Time Employment in Europe, North America and the Pacific Rim*. London: Routledge, pp. 177–198.

Plantenga, J. (2002). 'Combining work and care in the polder model: an assessment of the Dutch part-time strategy', *Critical Social Policy*, 22: 1, 53–71.

Polanyi, K. (1957). *The Great Transformation*. New York: Rhinehart.

Pollert, A. (2010). 'The lived experience of isolation for vulnerable workers facing workplace grievances in 21st-century Britain', *Economic and Industrial Democracy*, 31: 1, 62–92.

Proctor, S. (2006). 'Organizations and organized systems: from direct control to flexibility', in S. Ackroyd, R. Batt, P. Thompson and P. S. Tolbert (eds) *The Oxford Handbook of Work and Organizations*. Oxford: Oxford University Press, pp. 462–484.

Ramsay, H. (1977). 'Cycles of control: worker participation in sociological and historical perspective', *Sociology*, 11: 3, 481–506.

Raven, B. H. (1992). 'A power/interaction model of interpersonal influence: French and Raven thirty years later', *Journal of Social Behaviour and Personality*, 7: 2, 217–244.

Rawlinson, K. (2017). 'Judge calls for clarity on status of ECJ rulings in UK after Brexit', *Guardian*. Available at: www.theguardian.com/politics/2017/aug/08/judge-calls-for-clarity-on-status-of-ecj-rulings-in-uk-after-brexit. [Accessed 20 May 2019].

Resolution Foundation, The (2017). 'A tough gig? The nature of self-employment in 21st century Britain and policy implications'. Available at: www.resolutionfoundation.org/publications/a-tough-gig-the-nature-of-self-employment-in-21st-century-britain-and-policy-implications/. [Accessed 1 August 2017].

Rifkin, J. (2014). *The Zero Marginal Cost Society*. New York: Palgrave Macmillan.

Roberts, M. (2016). 'Can robots usher in a socialist utopia or only a capitalist dystopia?', *Socialist Review*, July/August. Available at: http://socialistreview.org.uk/415/can-robots-usher-socialist-utopiaor-only-capitalist-dystopia. [Accessed 3 May 2018].

Robinson, P. (1999). 'Exploring the relationship between flexible employment and labour market regulation', in A. Felstead and N. Jewson (eds) *Global Trends in Flexible Labour*. Basingstoke: Macmillan, pp. 84–89.

Rogers, J. and W. Streeck (1995). 'The study of works councils: concepts and problems', in J Rogers and W. Streeck (eds) *Works Councils: Consultation, Representation, and Cooperation in Industrial Relations*. Chicago: University of Chicago Press, pp. 3–26.

Romei, V. (2017). 'How wages fell in the UK while the economy grew', *Guardian*. Available at: www.ft.com/content/83e7e87e-fe64–11e6–96f8–3700c5664d30. [Accessed 2 March 2019].

Rose, J. B. (1986). 'Legislative support for multi-employer bargaining: the Canadian experience', *Industrial and Labor Relations Review*, 40: 1, 3–18.

Rowley, C. and K. S. Bae (2013). 'Waves of anti-unionism in South Korea', in G. Gall and T. Dundon (eds) *Global Anti-Unionism: Nature, Dynamics, Trajectories and Outcomes*. London: Palgrave, pp. 207–223.

Royal Commission on Trade Unions and Employers' Associations (1968). 1965–1968 Cmnd. 3623. London: HMSO.

Royle, T. (2010). 'The ILO's shift to promotional principles and the "privatisation" of labour rights: an analysis of labour standards, voluntary self-regulation and social clauses', *International Journal of Comparative Labour Law and Industrial Relations*, 26: 3, 249–271.

Rubery, J. (1978). 'Structured labour markets, worker organisation and low pay', *Cambridge Journal of Economics*, 2: 1, 17–36.

Rubery, J. (2005). 'Labour markets', in A. Ackroyd, R. Batt, P. Thompson and P. Tolbert (eds) *A Handbook of Work and Organization*. Oxford: Oxford University Press, pp. 31–51.

Rubery, J. (2011). 'Reconstruction amid deconstruction: or why we need more of the social in European social models', *Work, Employment & Society*, 25: 4, 658–674.

Rubery, J. (2015). 'Change at work: feminisation, flexibilisation, fragmentation and financialisation', *Employee Relations*, 37: 6, 633–644.

Rubery, J. and C. Fagan (1995). 'Comparative industrial relations research: towards reversing the gender bias', *British Journal of Industrial Relations*, 33: 2, 209–236.

Rubery, J. and G. Hebson (2018). 'Applying a gender lens to employment relations: revitalisation, resistance and risks', *Journal of Industrial Relations*, 60: 3, 414–436.

Rubery, J., A. Keizer and D. Grimshaw (2016). 'Flexibility bites back: the multiple and hidden costs of flexible employment policies', *Human Resource Management Journal*, 26: 3, 235–251.

Rubery, J., D. Grimshaw, A. Keizer and M. Johnson (2018). 'Challenges and contradictions in the "normalising" of precarious work', *Work, Employment and Society*, 32: 3, 509–527.

Ruddick, G. (2016). 'Tata Steel jobs: regulator warns of pension hurdles', *Guardian*. Available at: www.theguardian.com/business/2016/dec/08/port-talbot-steel-regulator-warns-pension-hurdles. [Accessed 10 May 2019].

Ruddick, G. (2017). 'McDonald's offers fixed contracts to 115,000 UK zero-hours workers', *Guardian*. Available at: www.theguardian.com/business/2017/apr/25/mcdonalds-contracts-uk-zero-hours-workers. [Accessed 20 May 2019].

Rushe, D. (2018). 'McDonald's workers walk out in 10 US cities over "sexual harassment epidemic"', *Guardian*. Available at: www.theguardian.com/business/2018/sep/18/mcdonalds-walkout-workers-protest-sexual-harassment-epidemic. [Accessed 20 June 2019].

Safi, M. (2018). 'Bangladesh to eject safety inspectors brought in after Rana Plaza disaster', *Guardian*. Available at: www.theguardian.com/world/2018/nov/28/international-inspectors-to-leave-bangladesh-after-factory-fire. [Accessed 3 February 2019].

Salehi, N., L. Irani, M. S. Bernstein, A. Alkhatib, E. Ogbe, K. Miland and Clickhappier (2015). 'We are Dynamo: overcoming stalling and friction in collective action for crowdworkers', 33rd Annual ACM Conference on Human Factors in Computing Systems, Seoul.

Schwab, K. (2016). *The Fourth Industrial Revolution*. Switzerland: World Economic Forum.

Sennett, R. (1998). *The Corrosion of Character: The Personal Consequences of Work in the New Capitalism*. London: W. W. Norton & Company.

Shambaugh, J., R. Nunn, P. Lui and P. Nantz (2017). 'Thirteen facts about wage growth', The Hamilton Project. Available at: www.brookings.edu/wp-content/uploads/2017/09/thp_20170926_thirteen_facts_wage_growth.pdf. [Accessed 1 May 2019].

Shildrick, T., R. MacDonald, A. Furlong, J. Roden and R. Crow (2012). 'Are "cultures of worklessness" passed down the generations?' Joseph Rowntree Foundation. Available at: www.jrf.org.uk/sites/files/jrf/worklessness-families-employment-full.pdf. [Accessed 1 May 2019].

Simms, M., J. Holgate and E. Heery (2012). *Union Voices: Tactics and Tensions in UK Organizing*. Ithaca: ILR Press.

Sisson, K. (2012). *Employment Relations Matters*. Warwick: Warwick Business School.

Skills for Care (2016). *The State of the Adult Social Care Sector and Workforce in England*. Leeds: Skills for Care. Available at: www.skillsforcare.org.uk/stateof2016. [Accessed 20 September 2017].

Slee, T. (2015). *What's Yours Is Mine: Against the Sharing Economy*. New York: OR Books.

Smith, D. and P. Chamberlain (2015). *Blacklisted: The Secret War between Big Business and Union Activists*. Oxford: New Internationalist Publications Limited.

Spencer, D. (2017). 'Work in and beyond the Second Machine Age: the politics of production and digital technologies', *Work, Employment and Society*, 31: 1, 142–152.

Srnicek, N. and A. Williams (2016). *Reinventing the Future: Postcapitalism and a World without Work*. New York: Verso.

Standing, G. (2011). *The Precariat: The New Dangerous Class*. London: Bloomsbury Academic.

Stewart, P. (2006). 'Marginal movements and minority struggles? The case of the Japanese minority social and labour movements', *The Sociological Review*, 54: 1, 753–773.

Stewart, P. and M. Martínez Lucio (2017). 'Research, participation and the neo-liberal context: The challenges of emergent participatory and emancipatory research approaches', *Ephemera* 17: 3, 533–556.

Stonewall (2017a). Available at: www.stonewall.org.uk/. [Accessed 20 November 2018].

Stonewall (2017b). *Stonewall Top 100 Employers*. Available at: www.stonewall.org.uk/sites/default/files/top_100_employers_2017-web.pdf. [Accessed 20 November 2018].

Storey, J. and N. Bacon (1993). 'Individualism and collectivism: into the 1990s', *International Journal of Human Resource Management*, 4: 3, 665–684.

Streeck, W. (2011). 'The crises of democratic capitalism', *New Left Review*, 71, 5–29.

Stuart, F., H. Pautz and S. Wright (2016). 'Decent work for Scotland's low-paid workers: a job to be done', Oxfam Partnership. Available at: www.uwsoxfampartnership.org.uk/wp-content/uploads/2014/10/Decent-Work-in-Scotland-Low-Paid-Workers-final-report-.pdf. [Accessed 1 May 2019].

Stuart, M. (2007). 'Introduction: the industrial relations of learning and training: a new consensus or a new politics?', *European Journal of Industrial Relations*, 13: 3, 269–280.

Stuart, M., J. Tomlinson and M. Martínez Lucio (2013). 'Women and the modernization of British trade unions: meanings, dimensions and the challenge of change', *Journal of Industrial Relations*, 55: 1, 38–59.

Tailby, S., A. Pollert, S. Warren, A. Danford and N. Wilton (2011). 'Underfunded and overwhelmed: the voluntary sector as worker representation in Britain's individualised industrial relations system', *Industrial Relations Journal*, 42: 3, 273–292.

Tapia, M. and G. Alberti (2018). 'Unpacking the category of migrant workers in trade union research: a multi-level approach to migrant intersectionalities', *Work, Employment and Society*, 33: 2, 314–325.

Taylor, M. (2017). 'Good work: the Taylor review of modern working prac-
    tices', UK Government. Available at: www.gov.uk/government/groups/
    employment-practices-in-the-modern-economy. [Accessed 10 May 2019].
Taylor, P. (2019). 'A band aid on a gaping wound: Taylor and modern work-
    ing practices', *New Technology, Work and Employment*, 32: 2, 100–105.
Taylor, P. and P. Bain (1999). ' "An assembly line in the head": work and
    employee relations in the call centre', *Industrial Relations Journal*, 30: 2,
    101–117.
Taylor, P. and P. Bain (2007). 'Reflections on the call centre: a reply to
    Glucksmann', *Work Employment and Society*, 21: 2, 349–362.
Teague, P. and J. Donaghey (2009). 'Why has Irish social partnership sur-
    vived?', *British Journal of Industrial Relations*, 47: 1, 55–78.
Thompson, P. (2003). 'Disconnected capitalism: or why employers can't
    keep their side of the bargain', *Work, Employment and Society*, 17: 2,
    359–378.
Thompson, P. (2013). 'Financialization and the workplace: extending and
    applying the disconnected capitalism thesis', *Work, Employment and
    Society*, 27: 3, 472–488.
Thompson, P. and S. Vincent (2010). 'Labour process theory and critical
    realism', in P. Thompson and C. Smith (eds) *Working Life: Renewing
    Labour Process Analysis*. UK: Palgrave Macmillan, pp. 47–69.
Tilly, C. (2011). 'The impact of the economic crisis on international migra-
    tion: a review', *Work, Employment and Society*, 25: 4, 675–692.
TUC (Trade Union Congress) (2008). 'Hard work, hidden lives: the full
    report of the commission on vulnerable employment'. Available at: www.
    vulnerableworkers.org.uk/files/CoVE_full_report.pdf. [Accessed   5
    May 2019].
TUC (Trade Union Congress) (2016). 'More than two-thirds of agency
    workers aged under 30 are looking for permanent jobs, says TUC'.
    Available   at: www.tuc.org.uk/economic-issues/labour-market-and-
    economic-reports/labour-market/economic-analysis/more-two-thirds
    [Accessed 1 March 2019].
TUC (Trade Union Congress) (2020). 'Protecting workers' jobs and
    livelihoods'. Available at: www.tuc.org.uk/research-analysis/reports/
    protecting-workers-jobs-and-livelihoods. [Accessed 11 May 2020].
TUC Digital (2019). 'Optimising digital engagement with union comms'.
    Available at: https://digital.tuc.org.uk/optimising-digital-engagement-
    with-union-comms/#more-293. [Accessed 20 June 2019].
UNCTAD (United Nations Conference on Trade and Development)
    (2011). 'World investment report'. Available at: www.unctad.org/
    en/pages/PublicationWebflyer.aspx?publicationid=84.   [Accessed   11
    July 2019].

Van den Broek, D. and T. Dundon (2012). '(Still) up to no good: reconfiguring the boundaries of worker resistance and misbehaviour in an increasingly unorganised world', *Relations Industrielles/Industrial Relations*, 67: 1, 97–121.

Van den Broek, D., W. Harvey and D. Groutsis (2015). 'Commercial migration intermediaries and the segmentation of skilled migrant employment', *Work, Employment and Society*, 30: 3, 523–534.

Van Wanrooy, B., H. Bewley, A. Bryson, J. Forth, S. Freeth, L. Stokes and S. Wood (2011). 'The 2011 workplace employment relations study: first findings', WERS. Available at: www.gov.uk/government/publications/the-2011-workplace-employment-relations-study-wers. [Accessed 15 July 2019].

Van Wanrooy, B., H. Bewley, A. Bryson, J. Forth, S. Freeth, L. Stokes and S. Wood (2013). *Employment Relations in the Shadow of Recession: Findings from the 2011 Workplace Employment Relations Study*. Basingstoke: Palgrave Macmillan.

Verma, A. and T. A. Kochan (1985). 'The growth and nature of the non-union sector within a firm', in T. A. Kochan (ed.) *Challenges and Choices facing American Labor*. Boston: MIT Press, pp. 89–117.

Virdee, S. and K. Grint (1994). 'Black self-organization in trade unions', *The Sociological Review*, 42: 2, 202–226.

Visser, J. (2002). 'The first part-time economy in the world: a model to be followed?', *Journal of European Social Policy*, 12: 1, 23–42.

Vosko, L. F. (2010). *Managing the Margins*. Oxford: Oxford University Press.

Walden, R. M. (2013). 'Controversial new fees, revised tribunal rules and lower cap for most on unfair dismissal compensation', *Business Law Review*, 34: 5, 195–197.

Wedderburn, L. (1986). *The Worker and the Law*. Harmondsworth: Penguin.

Weil, D. (2014). 'Fissured employment: implications for achieving decent work', in D. McCann, L. Sangheon, P. Belser, C. Fenwick, J. Howe and M. Lueker (eds) *Creative Labour Regulation*. Basingstoke: Palgrave Macmillan, pp. 35–62.

Weiss, M. (2013). 'International labour standards: a complex public–private policy mix', *International Journal of Comparative Labour Law and Industrial Relations*, 29: 1, pp. 7–20.

Whittall, M., H. Knusden and F. Huijen (2009). 'European works councils: identity and the role of information and communication technology', *European Journal of Industrial Relations*, 15: 2, 167–185.

Wilkinson, A., T. Dundon and I. Grugulis (2007). 'Information but not consultation: exploring employee involvement in SMEs', *International Journal of Human Resource Management*, 18: 7, 1279–1297.

Wilkinson, A., T. Dundon, J. Donaghey and R. B. Freeman (2020). 'Employee voice: bridging new terrains and disciplinary boundaries', in A. Wilkinson, J. Donaghey, T. Dundon and R. B. Freeman (eds) *Handbook of Research on Employee Voice*, 2nd edition. Cheltenham: Edward Elgar, pp. 2–18.

Willcocks, L. and M. Lacity (2016). *Service Automation: Robots and the Future of Work*. London: Steve Brooks Publishing.

Williams, S. and P. Scott (eds) (2016). *Employment Relations under Coalition Government: The UK Experience, 2010–2015*. London: Routledge.

Wills, J. (2012). 'The geography of community and political organisation in London today', *Political Geography*, 31: 2, 114–126.

Wills, J., K. Datta, Y. Evans, J. Herbert, J. May and C. McIlwaine (2009). 'Religion at work: the role of faith-based organizations in the London living wage campaign', *Cambridge Journal of Regions, Economy and Society*, 2: 3, 443–461.

Wilshaw, R., C. Do Quynh, P. Fowler and T. Pham Thu (2016). 'Labour rights in Vietnam: Unilever's progress and systemic challenges', Oxfam Research Reports. Available at: www.policy-practice.oxfam.org.uk/publications/labour-rights-in-vietnam-unilevers-progress-and-systemic-challenges-614926. [Accessed 3 June 2019].

Wilson, T., L. Gardiner and K. Kasnowski (2013). 'Work in progress: low pay and progression in London and the UK', Centre for Economic and Social Inclusion. Available at: www.trustforlondon.org.uk/publications/work-progress-low-pay-and-progression-london-and-uk/. [Accessed 20 March 2019].

Winner, L. (1980). 'Do artefacts have politics?', *Daedalus*, 109: 1, 121–136.

Wolf, M. (2004). *Why Globalization Works*. Yale: Yale University Press.

Wood, J. (2016). 'Coworker.org: a platform for worker voice', TUC Digital. London: Trades Union Congress. Available at: https://digital.tuc.org.uk/coworker-org-platform-worker-voice/. [Accessed 30 August 2019].

Wood, J. (2019). 'Campaigning to win with digital: TUC Digital Lab workshop report', TUC Digital. London: Trades Union Congress. Available at: https://digital.tuc.org.uk/campaigning-to-win-with-digital-tuc-digital-lab-workshop-report/. [Accessed 10 July 2019].

Woolfson, C. and J. Sommers (2006). 'Labour mobility in construction: European implications of the Laval un Partneri dispute with Swedish labour', *European Journal of Industrial Relations*, 12: 1, 49–68.

Worksmart (2018). Available at: www.getworksmart.co.uk/. [Accessed 11 August 2019].

Wright Mills, C. (1948). *The New Men of Power: America's Labor Leaders*. New York: Augustus M. Kelly.

Zwick, D. (2015). 'Defending the right lines of division: Ritzer's prosumer capitalism in the age of commercial customer surveillance and big data', *Sociological Quarterly*, 56: 3, 484–498.

Index

Advisory, Conciliation and
    Arbitration Service (ACAS)
    xiii, 100, 105, 117
alienation, of work ix, 1
austerity 31, 73, 85

Brexit 100

Citizens Advice Bureau 59, 92
civil society organisations 76, 81
    external advisory organisations 92
    interest-based representative 93
    mobilising social movements 94
    networking agencies 94
    and voice 90–91
class 24, 33
collective bargaining 46, 50, 55, 56,
    71, 86, 102
    and coverage vi, 86, 87
    and equality 102
    and floor of rights 113
    politics and power 85
contract of employment 52–56, 60,
    61, 66
    'worker' definition 61, 62, 64
COVID-19
    front line workers 1
    furloughed workers 86

government responses 27, 86
    homeworking 110
    the role of the state 106
    self-employed 27
    and trade union influence 86,
    111

decentralisation 21, 50
Department of Business
    Innovation and Skills 55
discrimination x, 38, 54, 55, 59,
    62, 67

employee voice 46
    double breasting 89
    'efficiency-equity-voice'
    framework 12
    and the state 50, 51
    and women 73
equality 11, 12, 14, 30, 44, 45, 114
European Directive on *Employee
    Information and Consultation* 78
European Union 50, 51, 53, 57, 78

financialisation ix, 17
    and capitalism 25–26
flexibility 28, 31, 37, 46, 72, 102, 103
    see also fragmentation of work

fragmentation of work 27–31
frames of reference 12, 16

gender equality
    and change 70–71
    and regulation 66–67
    and work-life balance 71–74
gig economy 14, 18, 36, 44, 63, 65
globalisation
    and capitalism 23–25

health and safety 3, 77, 97

imbalance of bargaining power 54,
    56, 64
International Labour Organisation
    (ILO) 3, 13, 56, 100
internet 110
involvement and participation *see*
    employee voice

joint consultative committees
    78–80
    see also employee voice

labour markets 22, 23, 39, 72, 102
labour migration and power 67–70
    permit system 68
    Posted Workers' Directive 69
labour mobilisation x, 20, 94, 95,
    113
labour rights
    collective rights 46, 56, 75, 107
    individual rights 56, 75, 100
living wage campaigns 94–97
low pay 33, 36

multinational corporations 3, 23, 24

neoliberalism 46, 50, 68, 80, 105,
    112

new technology
    artificial intelligence x, 5, 40,
        104, 106
    digital platforms 36–39
    robotics and the future of work
        39–42
    and work 26–27
non-standard forms of employment
    31–36

outsourcing 14, 28, 33, 102

parties 19
pay 20, 33, 60, 63, 70, 71, 89
poverty 43, 48, 111
power
    definition 2
    frameworks 4–9
precarious work x, 14, 15, 21, 33,
    42, 90, 95
privatisation 106

race 21, 47

self-employed 22, 31, 64, 73
self-employment 30
    bogus contracts x, 14, 31, 63, 102
solidarities
    collective power 16
    collective solidarities 9
    vicious circle 8, 36
    virtuous circle 7
state
    deregulation 50–52
    dysfunctional state 49–50
    the role of the state 45–47
    social character of the state
        48–49
strike 20, 69, 81
subcontracting 21, 28, 29, 33,
    36, 43

supra-national legal forces
 employment tribunals 58, 71
 Equality Act 57
 EU social and employment
  legitlation 57
 Trade Union Act xi, 20, 55, 56,
  90, 102

trade unions 88–97, 109, 111, 113,
 114
 decline 18, 20

union avoidance 88–90
union organising 90–91

union voice and power 80–84
 see also employee voice
union-management partnerships
 84–85
 see also employee voice

work and employment studies
 (WES)
 core dimensions 14
 definitions 9–11
works councils *see* employee voice
 76–78

zero-hours work 28–33